From the
to the Armistice

The Memoirs of
Captain Stormont Gibbs, MC

Edited by
Richard Devonald-Lewis

With a Foreword by
The Rt Hon Enoch Powell
MBE, MA, MP

GLIDDON BOOKS
NORWICH, NORFOLK

First published in 1986 by William Kimber
Reissued in 1992 by Gliddon Books

© Richard Devonald-Lewis, 1986 and 1992

ISBN 0 947893 26 1

Printed by Antony Rowe, Chippenham, Wiltshire

Contents

Acknowledgements

I should like to express my thanks to Vera Rose (for many years secretary to Stormont Gibbs) for all the help she gave me in preparing this book, not least in typing and re-typing the manuscript, to my friend Anne Parsons who read it in its formative stages and offered invaluable advice, and to Gillian Kizintas who also gave great help.

My thanks are also due to Mr G. T. Sassoon for permission to quote from the works of Siegfried Sassoon, to Messrs A. P. Watt to quote from 'Elegy in a Country Churchyard' and 'For a War Memorial' by G. K. Chesterton, and to the Trustees of the Suffolk Regimental Museum for extracts from *The History of the Suffolk Regiment, 1914–1927*, by Lt-Colonel C. C. A. Murphy.

R.D.-L.

To Stormont Gibbs and his comrades in arms,
in recognition and gratitude
for their fortitude and sacrifice
and to my son
Owen
in the hope.that he will never
have to endure the same.

R.D.-L.

Foreword

by
The Rt Hon Enoch Powell,
MBE, MA, MP

Those who wore the King's coat in the Second World War can never wholly free themselves from a haunting doubt : could we have done and endured what those before us did and endured in the First World War? The remarkable document which Richard Devonald-Lewis has prevented from being lost and has brilliantly presented and edited suggests a partial answer to our question, a half-resolution of our self-doubt. The document is remarkable because the man who wrote it in pencil on school exercise books in 1930 was writing with no idea that it would ever be published but because of an inner compulsion to ease the burden of harrowing memories by committing them to paper.

Individually, the men who fought on the Somme and at Arras were just like ourselves, with the normal proportion of cowards, impostors, fools, buffoons, incompetents and heroes – above all, of cowards, the cowards who run and the cowards who take care never to go where there is cause to run. It was the memory of human inadequacies that Captain Gibbs of the 4th Suffolk was constrained to externalise in a direct, unvarnished narrative of irresistible sincerity.

> The young and brave, the strong and sure,
> The true, the upright and the pure,
> The thief, the coward, the perjurer,
> The cuckold, the adulterer,
> The men that stood, the men that fled,
> They all are here, and all are dead.

'Twas not because he thought it well
That any of them fought and fell;
Far other would have been their choice,
If fate had given them a voice;
But mastered by the might of chance,
They flocked to perish here in France.*

No sooner, however, do we of World War II settle into a comforting reassurance that we and they of World War I were much the same, the same selection of standard specimens of the human species, than the spectre of our old doubt rises again in a new guise with redoubled menace. It runs now: could the British nation ever again do and endure what it did and endured between 1914 and 1918 – above all, between 1916 and 1918? Individually we are the same perhaps; but are we the same collectively?

Of course in the First War there were strikes, there were mutinies, there were mass failures of nerve among the British; but still it remains staggering and incomprehensible how the nation yielded up its youth and its manhood with such conviction, such lack of doubt or hesitation, as it continued to do long after the realities of trench warfare were indisputable in terms of casualty lists and eye-witness accounts.

I can only depose what I know. Those who came forward to enlist in the late 1930s believed they were volunteering for a continuation of 1916–18, for the same conditions of war and the same chances of survival as Captain Gibbs had so poignantly committed to paper. So I guess it may after all have been the same nation that went back to war in 1939. What I cannot guess, but can only hope, is that it is the same nation still.

J. ENOCH POWELL

* 'From a War Cemetery', *First Poems*, Enoch Powell (1937).

Preface

This is the story of a man and a few hundred of his fellow country-
men who in their youth were precipitated into a hell on earth beyond
the comprehension of all who did not share the experience or those
who possess almost supernatural powers of imagination. Through it
the virtues of valour, duty and honour triumph over cowardice and
extreme human degradation thanks to the corporate spirit of a
uniquely British institution – a great county regiment. These young
men were arguably the finest and most promising generation ever
raised in this country. Certainly their hopes and expectations of a
brave new world seemed solidly based until Armageddon struck in
1914.

It is ironic, just because the events of the Great War did happen
and, therefore, this is a true story, that the imagination is the more
tempted to question its credibility.

The 1st July 1916 was a watershed date in the history of the
British Army, and a date on which one can conveniently in retrospect cut the First World War into two halves, before and after.

Before was the period of hope and preparation for the eager junior
partner in the military alliance, after came grim disillusionment and
untold slaughter as the British Empire increasingly shouldered the
mantle (at times almost single-handed) of Germany's principal
adversary.

I have written this short story of the 4th Suffolk from the Somme
battles to the Armistice around the war memoirs (written, it would
appear, about twelve years after the war) of Captain Charles Cobden
Stormont Gibbs, MC, MA, Headmaster of Gayhurst Preparatory
School, Gerrards Cross, until his death in 1969. Born on 5th June

7

1898, he was the elder of the two sons of A. C. Gibbs of Hoppey Hall, Upminster, Essex. Educated at Radley he was commissioned into the Suffolk Regiment in December 1915.

A shy, unworldly and retiring man to all except the generations of schoolboys to whom he devoted the remaining fifty years of his life after the war, he was, like the flower of his generation, the classic, quiet English gentleman. With a naturally reserved temperament deeply scarred by the terrible events of these two years, he often appeared awkward and unapproachable to nearly all except his boys, so it is not surprising that his notes on his war experiences (written in pencil in school exercise books) were shown to but a few in his lifetime.

After twelve years his memory had played him false on one or two details which reference to the official war diary of the battalion has been able to correct, but as far as possible I have left unaltered his own words – they speak for themselves. Some of the names, however, I have changed. Facts are corrected in notes at the end of each chapter. All that I, one of his former pupils, have attempted to do is briefly to expand on the history of his battalion[1] and its service in the context of the war as a whole, by way of providing a backdrop to his own narrative.

NOTE

[1] There is a personal diary covering the history of the battalion from the 2nd August 1914 to 21st May 1916 written by Lt-Col F. W. Turner, TD. It is available at both the Imperial War Museum and the Regimental Museum at Bury St Edmunds.

Prologue

The 4th Battalion[1] the Suffolk Regiment (the 12th of Foot) was a territorial battalion and the outbreak of war found them at their annual camp at Great Yarmouth. They immediately mobilised and moved to take up shore defence positions at Felixstowe.

The first night was full of incidents, humorous in retrospect. The golf course clubhouse was fortified, the windows being smashed and sandbagged, whilst sentries with fixed bayonets were placed along the sea shore to await the arrival of the German High Seas Fleet. One officer doing a round of inspection was fired at by a nervous and trigger-happy young 'terrier' and numerous worthy citizens of Felixstowe taking their customary late summer evening stroll across the links were arrested as German spies.

In miniature it well illustrated Britain's totally amateur approach and virtual total unpreparedness for participation in a great continental war. Blissfully, very, very few appreciated it at the time, because for these young Suffolk 'terriers' a terrible reality loomed ahead.

A territorial soldier was under no obligation for service overseas, but because of the appalling casualties in the Regular Army in the first four months of the war, at Mons, Le Cateau, the Marne, the Aisne and the 1st Battle of Ypres, the War Office called upon the Territorial Army to volunteer to join the BEF, by now in Flanders.

The response to this call in the 4th Suffolk was overwhelming and the battalion landed in France on 9th November 1914 eight companies strong[2] and saw their first action at Beuvy in December. Unaware that the war had another four years and two days to last, they landed in typically buoyant and jubilant mood, eager to 'have a go' before it was all over. Indeed the mood was immortalised by Charles Sorley, himself destined to die at Loos the following year as a captain in the 7th Battalion of the Suffolk Regiment.

> All the hills and vales along
> Earth is bursting into song,
> And the singers are the chaps
> Who are going to die perhaps.
>   O sing, marching men.
>   Till the valleys ring again.
>   Give your gladness to earth's keeping,
>   So be glad, when you are sleeping.

Nineteen-fifteen saw the battalion sustain heavy casualties at Neuve Chapelle, fight at Ypres, Arras and Loos as well as performing the normal 'line duties'. By July 1916 they had moved to the Somme sector under the command of Lieutenant-Colonel H. C. Copeman, DSO (late of the Essex Regiment) as part of 98 Brigade in the 33rd Division. Of the men who had landed with the 4th Suffolk twenty-one months before, only a bare handful remained. Colonel Copeman was the fourth CO. Of the previous three one had been killed and the other two invalided home with wounds.

NOTES

[1] After the 1908 Haldane reforms the 1st and 2nd battalions of a regiment were Regular battalions, the 3rd and 4th Territorial. In the Great War subsequent battalions raised took succeeding numbers.

[2] At this time a battalion normally had only four companies.

CHAPTER ONE

The Somme

In the early hours of Saturday, 1st July 1916, an atmosphere of tense expectancy hung over the British trenches in the Somme sector of the Western Front, as hundreds of thousands of young men – the very cream of the British Empire – waited for the commencement of the greatest battle the British Army had ever fought.

For seven days shells (approximately 1,600,000 of them) had screamed overhead, pulverising the German trenches and defences with such destructive power that both man-made obstacles to a victorious advance and indeed the human enemy themselves should have by now been totally obliterated; at least this was what had been calculated by the generals and their staffs.

When the artillery barrage lifted and the huge mines dug under the enemy front line trenches had been blown, over a hundred thousand enthusiastic soldiers were to go 'over the top' and slowly advance, with fixed bayonets, rifles at the high port, in perfect formation, and occupy the enemy positions to their front. Then succeeding waves would probe forward and open up the great breach in the line through which, spearheaded by the cavalry, the British Army would pour and end the war.

This much the soldier knew, and his own part of it.

Britain and her Empire had waited nearly two years for this day. Having taken up the challenge of the Kaiser's Imperial Militarism the nation had grimly come to the realisation that early optimistic forecasts of it all being 'over by Christmas' (1914) were sadly and terribly ill-founded; and that John Bull was going to have to put his shoulder to the wheel as never before to put this strutting

Continental Prince and his ridiculous son[1] firmly in their place.

The Regular Army as constituted in 1914 – the Old Contemptibles – which won immortal glory in the battles of 1914 and early 1915, had been decimated. The original Territorial Army had followed them to the grave and now, whilst, like the Regular Army, it recruited independently, had very few men in its ranks who had worn uniform in 1914.

The most famous recruiting poster in history, Lord Kitchener's stern glance, staring eyes and pointed finger, had produced Britain's Volunteer Army to fill the gap in the field, but for two years it had trained and equipped and few of 'Kitchener's Army' had as yet been in full scale battle.[2] The main brunt of the land fighting had been borne by our allies France and Russia.

Only at sea had the might of the Royal Navy imposed a strangling blockade upon Germany and the Central Powers, chased their commerce from the seas and taken soldiers to strip them of their colonial possessions. Indeed only six weeks before at Jutland had it been clearly demonstrated that despite some unpleasant lessons learnt about some inadequacies of our naval gunnery, Britannia still firmly ruled the waves.

Now things were different. The British Empire had mobilised, and to an extent, bearing in mind its essentially non-military nature, that was truly astonishing. Vast volunteer armies stood on the soil of France backed by the resources of the greatest geographical and industrial empire the world had ever seen, and those resources were now geared to total war.

Not that the mood of the troops was the same jingoistic abandon that had marked the outbreak of war. In poetic terms, 'If I should die think only this of me' and 'Now, God be thanked Who has matched us with His hour' would no longer be an accurate barometer to the morale prevalent in the trenches. Rupert Brooke already lay in his Aegean grave, yet the savage bitterness personified by Siegfried Sassoon and others still lay in the future.

The army that awaited the order to assault was, in the opinion of many military experts since, the finest Britain ever had. In potential it almost certainly was, but meaningful comparisons

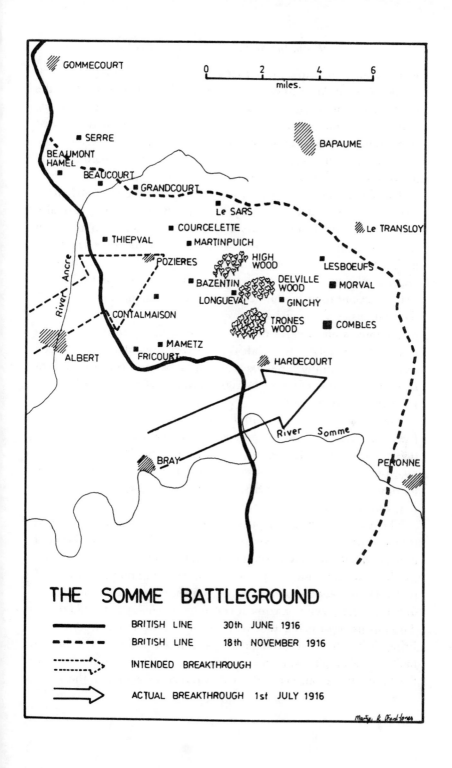

GOMMECOURT

0   2   4   6
miles.

SERRE

BAPAUME

BEAUMONT HAMEL

BEAUCOURT

GRANDCOURT

Le SARS

Le TRANSLOY

COURCELETTE

THIEPVAL

MARTINPUICH

HIGH WOOD

POZIERES

LESBOEUFS

River Ancre

BAZENTIN

DELVILLE WOOD

MORVAL

LONGUEVAL

GINCHY

CONTALMAISON

TRONES WOOD

COMBLES

MAMETZ

ALBERT

FRICOURT

HARDECOURT

River Somme

BRAY

PERONNE

THE SOMME BATTLEGROUND

——————   BRITISH LINE   30th JUNE 1916

– – – – –   BRITISH LINE   18th NOVEMBER 1916

· · · · ·►   INTENDED BREAKTHROUGH

⟹   ACTUAL BREAKTHROUGH 1st JULY 1916

Martin & Grandjones

against, say, the armies of Henry V, Cromwell, Marlborough, Wellington, Alexander or Montgomery, are not possible because the destiny of this army was to be slaughtered, not used. Like its predecessors only a skeleton was left upon which to attach the conscript armies who took the field the following year.

It was doubly tragic that the higher command never really appreciated the full potential of calibre of the men then under orders, but tended to think of them as just the same as the old hard-bitten tough regulars (immortalised by Kipling's Barrack Room Ballads). 'Enlisted for drink or worse' was how the Duke of Wellington described them. Many of them would freely admit that 'the army got them before the police did'; and thus this new force was deemed as unintelligent and to be kept in proper discipline by the strictest application of the Sergeant-Major's tongue and by King's Regulations.

Volunteers all, they came from every walk of life and from the length and breadth of the land. Whole streets and villages had joined up together, forming the same 'Pals' battalions and companies, with tragic consequences for whole neighbourhoods when these units were later decimated in battle.

Thus also was the 4th Suffolk. Men from the larger towns like Bury and Ipswich would compose whole companies and likewise those from the smaller centres like Sudbury and Hadleigh and the outlying villages would engineer or wangle themselves together, many serving under a young officer who would be the son of a local squire or gentleman whom they knew.[3]

The failures and disappointments of the previous two years had soured neither the nation nor its army. Indeed they had only inspired a quiet and deadly determination for final victory.

Thus this vast new army had drilled, trained and prepared itself with determination and confidence, blissfully ignorant of what lay ahead, of their own inadequacies or of those who were to lead them. The omens were good, the wealth of scholastic talent (indeed the Prime Minister's own brilliant scholar son was to die in this battle) had not hesitated to point out to all that was it not here by the Somme five hundred and one years before that Henry V had fought the battle of Agincourt, and was not the tremendous thunderstorm they had endured the night before exactly as it had been the night before Waterloo just one hundred and one years ago?

> Nor needs he any hearse to bear him hence,
> Who goes to join the men of Agincourt.
>
> Herbert Asquith

The host was young, eager and trusting.

*

The Higher Command's planning for the battle had commenced in late 1915. It had been calculated that with Germany fully committed on the Eastern Front the arrival of Kitchener's armies on the Western Front would produce such a superiority in numbers that 1916 would be the year in which to go on to the full scale offensive.

General Sir Douglas Haig, by now C-in-C of the BEF, favoured an attack in Flanders in conjunction with operations by the Royal Navy along the coast, with the objective of .capturing the Channel Ports in enemy hands and then commencing a great 'roll up' of the enemy's right flank. In this he was very much 'Neptune's General' and indeed the idea had great merits in the context of early 1916. However he failed to persuade either the Government or his Allies, and he was ordered to give whole-hearted co-operation to the plan devised by Marshal Joffre.

Throughout the Great War the British High Command, both political and military, seemed almost mesmerised by the belief that the French were the great masters of the military art and we the learners. Despite plenty of evidence already available that we had well learnt for ourselves, the Francophile cult lasted until the end of the war.

Joffre's plan envisaged a massive attack in which the British would be the smaller of the total forces employed. Planning would be meticulous, nothing would be left to chance and, in order to allow time for an overwhelming logistic build-up, a 'D' day was set for late July. So far so good, but when it came to the choice of ground the historian can see the writing appearing on the wall. He chose, it would appear, the Somme countryside purely because it was there the two Allied armies happened to shoulder each other at that time.

On the whole of the Western Front it is difficult to imagine an easier place for a numerically inferior but tenacious (and extremely expert in field fortifications) enemy to defend. The Somme region is open rolling chalk downland very similar to the southern slopes of Salisbury Plain in Wiltshire; indeed originally it was a continuation of the same geographical feature before the sea broke through forming the English Channel.

Here the Germans with great care had selected their defensive positions on the high ground, being quite prepared to yield a mile or so here and there to create the most perfect defensive position it was possible to achieve in the area.

It was said that the Somme was ideal cavalry country and so it was, but it was also machine-gun country and the German machine-gun positions were selected with great skill. It is fashionable nowadays for the ignorant to laugh at the 'Cavalry Generals' of the Great War. In 1916 the horse was still by far the most efficient method of land transport apart from a railway line, and one of the reasons why, when a breach in the line had been created (another myth is that the lines never were breached), it was always possible for the defenders, using their railway system (the Germans had the superior system) to bring reinforcements to the danger spot faster than the attackers could supply and reinforce their own forward troops. The age of mechanised warfare still lay in the future; the great gift of battlefield mobility it bestowed simply was not available to the generals of the Great War, and it is therefore wrong to scoff at generals who gave careful consideration to ground suited to mounted manoeuvre. No one was contemplating action like the Charge of the Light Brigade, but mounted men alone could swiftly exploit a breakthrough.[4] The 1st Battle of Ypres would have been lost but for the mobility of the cavalry regiments, who were ordered from one part of the line to another as circumstances dictated. Security, certainly by modern standards, was virtually non-existent, and virtually the only thing the Germans did not know was when the attack was coming; in the event even this information was handed to them on a plate.

However, all calculations were negated. For in February the German Army made their fearful onslaught on Verdun with the explicit intent (which to a large extent succeeded) of drawing the French Army to its graveyard, and by July the French contribution to the first day of the Somme offensive had shrunk to a mere five divisions on an eight mile front, thus reversing the roles of the Allied armies, with the British now becoming very much the major partner.[5]

Yet, despite the holocaust of Verdun, preparations proceeded as if nothing had happened; indeed it was even worse because Haig (and his staff), having resigned themselves to battle on the Somme and not Flanders, became both enthusiastic and ultra optimistic about the whole concept. This sense of optimism was to spread throughout the staff and the entire army and resulted in the former allowing themselves to be blinded to unpleasant realities right under their noses.

Much blame is heaped on the generals for what subsequently happened – a lot of it deservedly because Truman's truism 'the buck stops here' must always apply Yet much more should be heaped on their staffs who deliberately (indeed criminally, some would say) withheld unpleasant information from the senior commanders if it did not 'fit the plan'. For example, battalion officers who reported that the bombardment was not having the expected effect were even accused of cowardice.

The tactical idea was to create a break in the German line in the centre of the British armies' position on an axis Albert/Bapaume (Bapaume was a first day objective which had not even been taken when the battle was closed down four and a half months later) followed by a great wheel north. The duties of the French army on the right and the British left were to create diversionary attacks – no reserves were allocated or available for exploiting success in these sectors.

The front line deployment of both infantry and artillery was an even spread across the whole front, with no concentration on weak spots or even the intended point of breakthrough. Haig himself put forward two very intelligent tactical suggestions (which, if adopted, would have averted disaster and might even have brought victory): namely that there should be small probing attacks to test the actual state of the defences, and that when committed the infantry should rush their objectives.

However, the Army Commander in the centre, General Rawlinson (Fourth Army), had complete faith in the power of his artillery to obliterate all his objectives and the commonly held belief of all senior officers was that the new armies had not got either the battle experience or intelligence to regroup on their objectives, and thus they were ordered to keep perfect formation as they *walked* across no-man's land.

Haig, on the grounds that it was not the job of the overall commander to interfere with the tactical plans of the commander on the spot, and that Rawlinson, an infantryman, knew his job in this respect better than he, a cavalryman, did, did not unfortunately press his point. In retrospect we can see that he should have.

In deference to the French, who wanted perfect light for artillery observation, H hour was postponed till 7.30 a.m., thus throwing away the cloak of half-light that could have shielded the attacking infantry, each man of whom was laden with nearly 70lbs of equipment.

The final element of surprise was thrown to the wind. So anxious was one officer that the C-in-C's final order of the day should reach the front line troops that he broke orders and used a field telephone, which was tapped by the enemy, thus giving them the exact time of the attack. This was further confirmed for them in the morning when, in order that a good moving film could be taken of one of the great mines that had been laid beneath the German front line, one of these was blown ten minutes early for the benefit of the camera crew. Few of the viewers who see the film every time there is a TV documentary on the Great War realise how many of our soldiers' lives that bit of pandering to the home propaganda machine cost.

The only mitigating factor was both unasked for and undeserved in that the German High Command for their part remained convinced that this was only a very large diversionary attack and that the main blow would fall in Flanders. Indeed it was not until the battle was nearly a week old that the penny finally dropped with General Von Falkenhayn that this was no side-show.

The actual date was changed several times, being brought forward several weeks in response to French appeals to take the pressure off them at Verdun. Again at the last minute, for logistic reasons, the assault was postponed 48 hours. This resulted in the assaulting infantry who had already moved into the forward trenches having to wait in them in considerable discomfort for two days, and the artillery slackening their bombardment to spread the allocation of shells over seven rather than five days.

The First Day

Finally at 7.30 a.m. on 1st July the bombardment ceased, the great mines were blown with a roar that was heard in London and with (almost universal)[6] confidence to the sound of bugles, the skirl of the pipes, hunting horns, football rattles, accordions and many other instruments (A Company of the East Surreys even kicked four foot-balls before them)[7] the flower of the British Army went 'over the top' and advanced across no-man's land in exemplary formation. The previous night's thunderstorm had given way to a perfect July morning.[8]

However, in most places the bombardment had failed. Nearly everywhere the German wire had not been cut and blown clear, and the German front line troops were not dead. They had dug them-selves into shelters forty feet below the ground, a fact which British patrols had reported but which the staff had failed to pass on to the High Command, presumably on the basis that it would not be nice to upset the generals' breakfast with unpleasant news.

As soon as the bombardment stopped they swarmed like so many angry bees to the surface bringing their machine-guns with them. Had the British made a full-scale charge they would undoubtedly have stormed their objectives before the machine-guns could be brought into action, and trapped their foe beneath ground. The order to advance at the walk decreed otherwise.

Suddenly the machine-guns opened fire and, like ripened corn falling to the scythe, the British ranks began to fall, yet nowhere was the attack called off, and wave after wave followed to share the fate of their predecessors.

Only at the junction of the British and French armies was there success and a four mile break actually made in the enemy's defences. Again on the extreme left flank, the British (Third Army – General Allenby) actually took some of their diversionary objectives for a few hours. In neither place had success been planned for, in neither were there reserves available and a combination of primitive communications and total lack of flexibility in the plan resulted in the failure to take advantage of either situation. The great military maxim of 'reinforce success, not failure' rarely seemed to be understood by the generals of all armies in the Great War.

On the majority of the eighteen mile front the attack was a total and bloody failure. By the time the sun had reached its zenith nearly sixty thousand British soldiers lay dead or wounded. The majority in no-man's land.

The four and a half month battle of the Somme, which was to capture at most seven miles of ground (lost in a morning in March 1918), at a cost to the British alone of nearly half a million casualties, had begun. The 1st July 1916 was the greatest disaster ever to befall the British Army on the field of battle. The whole battle was, in the words of Sir Basil Liddell Hart, 'The glory and the graveyard of Kitchener's Army'.

NOTES

1 Crown Prince Wilhelm, laughingly known to the British as 'Little Willy'.

2 A few had fought at Gallipoli.

3 Indeed the principal character of this book, C. C. S. Gibbs, who was not a Suffolk man, enlisted with this battalion because his friend and study companion at Radley (C. P. Parry-Crooke) did hail from a landowning family in the county which had connections with the battalion. To have gone to war, other than together, would have been unthinkable.

4 On the day a break four miles wide *was* made, but not in the place planned for or expected by the staff. Had the planning been flexible enough to have allowed the cavalry to exploit it the story might have had a different ending.

5 Indeed in the event the British contribution was increased by four extra divisions.

6 Not everyone was oblivious to what was likely to happen – a battalion commander in the Middlesex Regiment committed suicide a few days later having failed to convince the staff of the fate awaiting his men. Captain Martin

of the Devons even constructed a model on which he marked with pin-point accuracy exactly where he and his men would die and the machine-gun that would kill them. They lie today in the Devonshires' cemetery at Mametz. The cemetery is particularly sombre as the date on every headstone is exactly the same : 1st July 1916.

[7] Two of these footballs can still be seen, one in the National Army Museum, the other in the Regimental Museum of the Queen's Division. A prize was to have been presented to the platoon who first kicked their ball into the German front line trench. It was never given, as the prizegiver, Captain Neville, fell himself that day.

[8] The searing heat of the day was one of the greatest agonies that the wounded, most without water, were later to endure.

Lt-Colonel H. C. Copeman DSO
Commanding Officer of the 4th Suffolk
Bn. (1917).

Captain C. C. S. Gibbs MC Adjutant to
the 4th Suffolk Bn. (1918).

Brigadier General J. D. Heriot-Maitland with staff officers, of 98 Brigade.

CHAPTER TWO

The Suffolks' Somme

Meanwhile, back in England 2nd Lieutenant Charles Cobden Stormont Gibbs, fresh from Radley and recently commissioned into the Suffolk Regiment, was with a training battalion at Halton :

Stormont Gibbs : One hot July day in 1916 we had been sent off for a route march round through Tring and the hills to the south. During an interval I was leaning over a farm gate talking with two or three junior officers and it was then that the telegram arrived to say I was to 'proceed overseas'. I do not remember being particularly interested except that it meant a week's leave first. We finished the march – some twenty miles – and I remember that I was carrying several rifles in addition to full pack and equipment for the last few miles. Strange to think how fit one must have been in those days. But I found puttees very trying to march in in summer.

[A few days later he was explaining to his parents during a riverside picnic near Abingdon :] that I was only going to France unexpectedly soon because we were to finish our training at a base camp 'near the sea' – it would be fun. The Colonel had said something of this sort : but it did not pan out like this. The real reason for officers being sent out, after only some six months' training, was the shortage caused by the enormous casualties in the Somme battle.

[He was sent to a base camp at Etaples ('Eat-Apples' or 'the Bull Ring' to the troops) where, needless to say, no training was done. This was the prelude for him to a short period of his life of which his recollections were :] so vivid for me that many of the events of this period stand out from the rest of my life in high relief and everything else seems in a far away mist by comparison with it. August 1916 might be a month or two ago. I can be more precise about most of it than anything I did last August. And as to the rest of the war, my mind is a blank except for incidents sufficiently stirring not to be completely thrown into shadow by the bright light of that August.

I have often wondered whether the process of describing minutely my sensations during that month would improve my memory in other respects – by getting rid of the thing as it were. That in fact is the reason for these notes.

[It is said that the human memory only really retains happy memories. For him, late July and August 1916 were obviously notable exceptions to this rule.]

After a few days in tents at Etaples, we were sent to join 1/4th Suffolk who were commanded by Lieutenant-Colonel H. C. Copeman, DSO.

Editor : The 4th Suffolk had been in the thick of the battle, making frontal assaults on the enemy on 15th and 20th July, the latter on the notorious High Wood. Their July casualties testify to the intensity of the fighting. Six officers were killed and fifteen wounded. The total other ranks' casualties were three hundred and thirty-three, or in other words over half the officers and nearly half the men.

Stormont Gibbs was part of a large replacement draft.

Stormont Gibbs : I remember the familiar sounds as we drew into Amiens station in the middle of the night and I remember also watching the familiar process of procuring hot water from the engine to make tea at the various lengthy stops. I am not at all clear about my companions; there were probably four of us and one was Norton. P-C had not come out yet nor Adams who was recovering from Scarlet Fever at Aylesbury.[1]

At Mirancourt, a small station on the Amiens–Albert line, we 'detrained'. This, I suppose, was the 33rd Division railhead and some twelve miles behind the front line. We were met by an officer of the battalion sent to fetch us, a certain Captain Hogg. He was a tall, strong, pleasant-looking man and I felt that here was one of the great men straight from the front line.

I had been much in awe of one captain when I first joined the reserve battalion at Halton. New young officers regarded him as a great hero and he was approached only by the more senior subalterns. In fact the difference between a senior and junior subaltern seemed to be a question of whether or not one 'knew' the captain. He had been out in France with the regiment in late 1914.

It was not till later that I found he had been in the front line for only a few hours if at all and that having safely got to England with an attack of measles he was taking good care to stay there by making himself indispensable to the colonel of the reserve battalion. He was always to the fore when it was a matter of taking the 'Old Man' to his house in Aylesbury after a thick night in the mess. It was not long before the captain with the help of some doughty partisans had turned a home battalion officer out of his feathered nest. He retained this nest, did the captain, until nearly the end of the war.

And here was another such captain I felt as I left the train at Mirancourt – but less unbending and evidently a great man. We spent the night at this village I fancy; though I don't know why and can't remember how.

My next recollection is that of reporting to the OC 4th Battalion Suffolk Regiment who were in tents at Dernancourt some eight miles behind the line. They were having a week's rest after losing half their officers and men at High Wood. It was apparently a risky thing to report to the Colonel at an unsuitable moment. We knew very few of the officers as all those who had gone out from Halton in the last few drafts had been killed. But a few kindly people welcomed us and held a meeting as to whether it was desirable that we should report to the Colonel at once or a little after his next meal. I developed an instinctive dread of this Colonel. But the Adjutant was roped in and he proved a most kindly fellow and assured us that all would be well and that we could go with him to see the 'Old Man'.

I suppose the interview with the Colonel was brief – I remember nothing about it. We heard a lot of the Colonel's likes and dislikes – that he objected to officers dressing like the men to avoid being picked off by snipers when they went over the top for instance. So I visited the QM sergeant and cancelled my order for a 'Tommy's tunic'.

I first came roughly into contact with the Colonel on parade next morning. I had been posted with Robertson to 'B' Company. The great Hogg was our company commander and possibly one of the other officers in the company was Cecil G. Sykes from whom I had bought a motor bike at Halton to my cost. I was a bit afraid of him – he had worked a rag on my stable companion at Halton though actually I had been passed over. We were all on parade I remember on a dusty trodden field; we must have had an exercise involving some open order work – probably to capture a mythical machine-gun behind a distant bank. I had sent off a sergeant with two sections to do something in this exercise and evidently in the Colonel's opinion this had been done all wrong for he was lecturing the battalion on the stupidity of Sergeant X and saying he could not have done in that way whatever it was he had been sent out to do.

At this point I called attention to my existence by shouting out that I had told the sergeant to do it like that and this alarming exhibition of my 'owning up' effectively cut short the Colonel's harangue. Sergeant X and my platoon probably began to form the opinion that I might be a suitable sort of young fool and doubtless no harm was done. The Colonel remarked that he would 'discuss the matter further with the officer later'. I don't remember his doing so but I certainly decided at once that his bark was worse than his bite and I ever after acted on that assumption on the many supremely trying occasions in later years – or rather months, for three months were like a year in those days – when I was his adjutant at variance with him.

On the evening of the first day at Dernancourt I was offered some whisky in a company mess and it made me feel sick – I'd never tasted it before, that I know of, and I mention this incident because it would be so odd nowadays for a young man never to have tasted whisky or beer. We scarcely realise how the public school grade of society has discovered the public house *since* the war and the pub has become a respectable resort.

But this evening of early August has left a greater impression on my mind for a reason other than my introduction to whisky as an essential part of an officer's equipment at the front. There was an officer named Pawsey. He had been at Halton and come out perhaps a fortnight before me[3] and having the good fortune to be posted to the reserve company had escaped the recent massacre at High Wood. In England he had appeared a fairly normal rather elderly subaltern – he was probably about thirty-four. I recalled he had recently married and had taken a house in Halton where his wife remained when he went abroad.

Now at Dernancourt this man seemed to have become the 'wag' of the battalion – a sort of funny-man-in-chief, so I thought, and it seemed to be curious. I commented on this to someone and he replied, oddly enough, 'Yes, the poor old chap', with a tone of genuine sympathy. I was puzzled. Soon I noticed that Pawsey was really odd and his behaviour was almost senile – the facetious punning banter more suitable to a man of seventy. I dimly comprehended then that this was a pose of his to 'hide his funk' as someone might have expressed it. I realise now his state of mind. To a mature man who could look on the war as it was – and not as we youngsters looked at it – it spelt almost certain death to be an infantry officer on the Somme at that moment. He could see his ten per cent chance of escape but like many I believe he knew that he had only a few days left to him and there, as he thought it all out, was the vision of his young wife. What man could not go crazy in this position and how typical this is of hundreds of other cases. War, death, prison may be a game for some and deep tragedy for others and yet we are all dished out with the same soup.

And there stood Pawsey cracking jokes outside his tent to keep up the spirits of us newcomers – for whom, most of us, there were no ties and only our parents standing to suffer for us. Within a week Pawsey had led his platoon to take a German trench. Half-way across he got a fatal bullet through the neck. But on he went and he took the trench and no one he knew ever saw him again.[4]

The weather at Dernancourt was hot – a real good heatwave – white roads and houses everywhere, there was no tar in those days. We were camped on the banks of the Ancre and the men bathed there. I can't remember why I did not, but I did go as a member of a water polo team to a village to play another battalion. I found I was not as fit as I thought I was nor as good at water polo. The recollection of my exhaustion and being very sick on the bank is still vivid!

A man got drowned in the Ancre one day. He had a funeral with chaplain and all. It struck me then as singular that there should be retained the pomp and circumstance of 'civilised' funerals within a few miles of where thousands were being killed and left in the mud. I suppose now that the ceremonies connected with such events as death, birth and marriage are still necessary to keep alive our ever weak sense of obligation and reverence for things beyond this world. But perhaps it is from the above incident that my repugnance to ceremony dates; the feeling that ceremonies though necessary are liable to be very hypocritical; that they originate as a means by which the governors may more easily manage the governed by playing on their superstitions and pandering to their love of pomp. Certainly this funeral struck me as unseemly. Why it seemed should there be a funeral parade over a man who was silly enough to drown himself? If it was of any value to the man surely we ought to be parading all day and all night for the assistance of the hundreds who had been killed and left lying about a few days before. Doubtless all right but incongruous!

Editor : The polo match was on 1st August – Minden Day. Whether all ranks were deeply conscious of the heroic dead of their regimental predecessors in 1759 we can only guess, but they were doubtless grateful that the anniversary was marked by a half holiday for all ranks and the polo match against the 2nd Battalion of the Regiment who were at Mericourt.

The fact that it was Minden Day was the first entry in the official war diary, which shows a proper British sense of perspective as to the relevant importance of the two wars. Three days later (the second anniversary of the beginning of their own war) the officers of the two battalions dined together – all very British and doubtless proper, but one can almost feel Stormont Gibbs' cynicism at such events at such a time.

During this period the battalion trained, and the war diary draws specific attention to a lecture from a captain in the RFC on 'Aeroplane signalling'.

The senior officers also reconnoitred 'trenches soon to be occupied'.

Fricourt Wood

Stormont Gibbs : A few days later we went up to 'Brigade in Support' at Fricourt Wood roughly three miles behind the line. And here begins 'my war'. (Probably 14th August[5].)

Fricourt Wood had not come off too badly. There were trees left with enough leaves to make some shelter from rain. Battalion HQ had a dug-out in the ditch but everyone else was in the open in different parts of the wood – sleeping, I suppose, on the ground on mac sheets but with no blankets or other kit. Strangely, I remember very little of the physical discomforts of the war.

Captain Hogg, Rash, Robertson and I were the officers of 'B' Company. Here for the first time my memory begins to be fresh. Sykes was battalion signalling officer and lived in the vicinity of Battalion HQ further off in the ditch – but not messing with the Colonel; only the 2nd i/c (when present) the Adjutant and MO ever had that honour throughout the war.

After food that evening the mail came and brought letters for me and a parcel. The parcel contained a 'bullet proof' body shield to go under a shirt, sent by my father. The fate of this article was humorous but there is too an element of pathos when one thinks of my father sending it off and his feelings then and my immediate decision that it would be far too hot to wear. Captain Hogg was not of the same opinion; could he try it on? Certainly. But he was a big man who took himself seriously and the sight of him in full armour was too much for his subalterns and some others less respectful from other companies. However, Captain Hogg had family ties – a good business on the Stock Exchange that could not spare him too long, certainly not indefinitely. In the end Captain Hogg had the longer back piece to wear on his front – and who could have imagined the great man being wounded except in front! and I kept the front piece to 'quis' to the highest bidder. Actually we used it for revolver practice a few weeks later and it nearly stood up to it. The history of the back bit on Hogg's front comes later.

That night we couldn't sleep because a wounded mule was screaming in the valley – there was only desultory shelling of the wood and only once near us. No one seemed to care about the mule but I got Norton to come with me to shoot it against Hogg's orders. However, it was dark and we could not find it. The noise ceased so I expect it died.

Editor: The war diary for 7th August reads: 'The battalion furnished a working party of 440 (110 from each Company) under 212 Company R. Engineers for digging "Thistle Alley" communication trench. This party was subjected to considerable hostile shelling. Casualties 1 other rank killed. 2nd Lieut. Sykes and 9 other ranks wounded.' Let the words of Stormont Gibbs elaborate on this bald statement of fact:

The Working Party

Stormont Gibbs: The work of digging new trenches and repairing old ones is done by one of the battalions in support. A brigade of four battalions would probably have two battalions in the front line, one in support, say, two miles back, and one in reserve a little further back. The brigade might remain 'in the line' for one or two weeks or more, the battalions taking it in turn to be in the front line. The reserve battalion might be in huts or tents or battered buildings and the idea was to rest it as far as possible. Similarly a battalion would probably have two companies (150 men odd each) in the front line trench and the other two in the support trench 100 yards or so behind. So that the actual number of companies used in the front line trench would be, say, four for a brigade of sixteen companies. The front line companies would alternate with those in support; thus with luck a man might not be in a front line trench for more than 48 hours consecutively. While in that trench the company would be responsible for sentry posts and firing positions along its line and for patrolling no-man's land and watching any enemy movements. It was not customary to 'pot' at an enemy should he show his head as this tended to attract reprisals and disturb the peace. In fact one only fought to orders, having I believe no feelings whatever of dislike for the enemy.

Now, the battalion in the line being fully occupied 'holding the front', it fell to the support battalion (normally resting) to furnish working parties each night. In the 4th Suffolk meals had to be punctual and if a man was digging all night he was liable to be expected for breakfast and parade at the normal hour so we seldom got rest in support. (This is probably an exaggeration except for those in close proximity to the CO.)

To return then to Fricourt Wood – 4th Suffolk Support Battalion of 98th Brigade : 1st Middlesex and 4th King's Liverpool in the line, 2nd Argylls in reserve. On the first night 'B' Company was to furnish a working party half-company strong. Hogg wasn't going and the other two officers, Robertson and myself had never seen a shell burst before that evening. Sykes was sent to the rescue from HQ. He took up the half-company to dig a communication trench, got wounded early on, and so nothing much got done.

Editor : For 8th August the war diary entry simply reads : 'Fricourt working party of 200 to 212 R.E. to continue "Thistle Alley" at 8 p.m.' Again Stormont Gibbs is able to add a lot to these few cold factual words :

Stormont Gibbs : So 'B' Company had to go again next night. Robertson and I went with an experienced sergeant who, Hogg said, would 'see us through' – Sergeant Baker. Robertson was a day senior to me so he was in charge.

Our instructions were to go via 'Death Valley' to Bazentin-le-Grand crossroads, there to meet a guide from the Royal Engineers at 1 a.m. (?) and take our instructions from him as to the position of the trench to be dug and the amount to be done. We should then space out our men and get on with it, leaving time to get back along the valley before dawn.

'Death Valley' today[6] looks an unassuming little piece of country with decaying dumps of barbed wire, boots and tin hats and shell noses alongside the farm track that runs along its southern side. From this track the land slips gently to the north for some 300 yards to the border of High Wood, the ground on which the brigade had been decimated a fortnight before when helping to drive back the enemy to the present front line some two miles on. On the south of the track was a hill rising in a series of terraces (some 30 feet) and in these terraces were old German dug-outs where men had cowered and others had thrown in bombs to mutilate them a week ago : and there were disused aid posts with here and there portions of a broken stretcher or the wheel from an ambulance. There were no dead as the ground had been cleared up.

So we started off along 'Death Valley' and had a mighty quiet journey considering the reputation of this mirky place – and not a casualty. In about an hour we rounded the hill and struck the Bazentin-le-Grand road turning south along it and before long there appeared the entrance to a CT[7] which ran along the right-hand ditch. After some fifteen minutes' slow progress along this trench the character of the evening changed. To one with more experience the quiet of the march up would have seemed sinister for the Somme, and now the enemy began to make up for it. The front line was now about half a mile on our left and our job doubtless was to repair (or dig another) trench from our present one to the front. The enemy knew we must make trenches here before we could launch another attack and it was their habit to bombard this ground in the early hours when working parties would be there. There came a large howling shell, then others in quick succession mostly out on our left, some very near our road. Up went the very lights along our front line to illuminate no-man's land in case the enemy were coming over. I stopped a moment to watch this beautiful sight and there on my left was High Wood, cold, bare skeletons of trees appearing and relapsing into the night with the light.

I was at the back and Robertson in front and a couple of minutes after the shelling started there was a halt for no apparent reason and no apparent intention of getting on in front. The men sat down wearily and put their shovels against the trench. Some grumbled that they couldn't light a pipe, others looked pale and tired and said nothing. Then there was the sound of voices ahead and someone saying 'make way' and Robertson appeared looking like a ghost. He flopped down by me and said, 'Oh Lord I can't stick this!' There had not been anything very evident to 'stick' but he was obviously finished and not likely to be any more use to anyone. So I gave him a swig of whisky from a flask and went up to the front line. Shells were falling on the road ahead. Was it my business to lead them on or wait ? How should I know ? Job to be done but lives to protect.

What did Sergeant Baker think? 'That's up to you, sir,' was all the help I got. 'Time we met the guide in five minutes about 200 yards on at the crossroad,' I said. 'Just where the shells are mostly falling,' he remarked dryly. 'Do you think the guide will be there?' I said. 'Never seen a RE guide near a shell yet,' said the sergeant. I decided to wait ten minutes to see if the shelling moderated. Meanwhile I walked back down the line to cheer people up and see how Robertson was. Half the men crouching down to get further from flying pieces of shell. Some, most I think, were exhausted and definitely terrified. I gave out a spot of whisky here and there to the youngest and most pasty-looking ones, a 'raw' sort of thing to do but I knew no better. Some of the way I walked in the road not for bravado but to show them the shelling wasn't too bad; they were mostly young recruits straight from England. Robertson was for going straight back but I knew we couldn't fail on two consecutive nights to dig that trench and I told him he could but the rest weren't yet awhile. Then I went to the front of the line again.

I took the party on 100 yards or so to within 100 yards of the crossroads. Then I halted them and went on alone to look for the guide. The shelling at the crossroads was only intermittent really – thick for a few minutes then five minutes with only a shell or two, often wide. I got out of the trench and had a look round. There was nothing but a large crucifix surrounded by blasted trees but apparently intact. It stands there today in a new grove of trees. First I stood in front of this and gazed at it and I thought, 'The Germans pray to Him too.' Then I turned down the road running west to the tiny village of Bazentin-le-Grand. Perhaps the guide was trying to shelter there. I came to the first house partially standing with a heap of rubble outside, and there I met a part of a man, but nothing to show if he had been an RE. It was a leg neatly severed above the knee, 'and the puttee is on the wrong way', I thought. 'What would the CO say if it came on parade?' The first time I had seen an unattached limb.

There was nothing else to be seen so I returned to the men. There was Sergeant Baker with a slight smile on his lips as much to say, 'So the silly young fool's back all right.' I didn't care for that man. 'We shall stay here for two hours,' I said, 'and I shall search for the guide every half hour. Now spread the men out so that an unlucky shell won't damage more than a few, and get a move on.' Sergeant Baker then got a move on and I had a rest.

We couldn't do anything useful without the guide and after two hours we returned and I wondered what the CO would say. He saw me and Sergeant Baker and I suppose that the sergeant then gave a good account of me for I got no blame. He didn't even say, 'I wish I'd sent so-and-so'. We had had one casualty, a twin brother killed, so I had to break the news to the other twin after breakfast and then I expect I slept, unaware of the blaspheming being hurled down telephone wires between battalions, brigades and divisions as a result of the failure of our guide to materialise. If the Army Staff had been even semi-intelligent they would have seen that more than one man knew details of the job to be done. I could have been told what was required and we should have dug some sort of trench somewhere. (I expect the brigade and division staffs had a bad breakfast that morning. The divisional general would have been woken up with the news that communications had not been completed. 'Whose fault?' '98th Brigade and the CRE.' 'Damn them, I shall lose my division at this rate,' he thinks, and then turning over for another nap : 'I don't think Smith ought to stay in command of that brigade.' Smith meanwhile wants to know why the hell Copeman couldn't get his blasted men to dig trenches – they come off the land in Suffolk. And Copeman was saying he suggested, 'Sir, that perhaps the fault lay with the RE organisation, sir.' And Smith was saying, 'Well, perhaps it is not your fault and anyhow what can you expect of Jones (the CRE), he never gets his orders out in time. But you know it looks bad for our brigade, Copeman.'

Editor : Several veterans have told me that personally they hated working parties more than pitched battles, as personified in Siegfried Sassoon's poem 'The Working Party'.

The battalion stayed in these trenches until moving up to relieve the 9th Battalion Highland Light Infantry in support on the 13th and then the 4th Battalion King's Liverpool Regiment in the front line on the 14th.

Up to Delville Wood

Stormont Gibbs: 'On August 18th the 33rd Division occupied the German positions at High Wood inflicting severe losses on the enemy. In some parts of the line we were unable to consolidate the newly won trenches owing to repeated counter-attacks and it was necessary to fall back a short way.'

Every statement like the above contains countless human stories of suffering and sacrifice. The following notes are about what happened to the 4th Suffolk Regiment.

On 16th August 1916 the 4th Suffolk moved from Brigade Support in Fricourt Wood to relieve the battalion holding the right half of the brigade's sector of the front line. It is possible that we started off about 9 p.m. and completed the relief about 1 a.m. but I remember nothing whatever about it. Probably the excitements of the working party the previous night are responsible for this blank in my memory.

We must have moved by the track up 'Death Valley' towards Bazentin-le-Petit. In the terrace which ran along the south edge of the track the Casualty Clearing Station (CRS) had been established in a large dug-out. This would be the most forward point for ambulances. It was about a mile along the valley to the N–S road joining Bazentin-le-Petit and Longueval. We would have moved with intervals between sections to minimise casualties from shell fire. And then we must have got into the trench we stuck in the night before and have worked along this for three-quarters of a mile to the Crucifix at the Bazentin-le-Grand crossroads. Here the proper communication trench began (the one we ought to have been digging at the previous night). It was about three-quarters of a mile long and led from the road in the valley eastwards to the ridge along which ran the front line trenches.

Progress up a rather battered CT is liable to be slow : it is only made for one-way traffic. People coming down have to flatten into a niche to let the relief go by and when it is a case of a stretcher coming down there is often a hold-up.

However, we completed the relief without incident and in what must have been very quick time for there was plenty of night left after it. 'B' Company was in the support trench some fifty yards behind the front line trench held by 'D' and 'C' Companies. 'A' Company was probably alongside us. Our Company HQ was a recess in the side of the trench covered by a piece of corrugated iron which should have kept off the rain. There were three scoops in the side of the recess making three seats, so Hogg, Robertson and I each had one and took it in turns to wander round looking at the men. We may have got a bit of sleep but I personally never became good at the cold and sitting-up kind and usually preferred to walk about. Such are the habits of man that during the warm part of the day when one might have slept one wasn't allowed to because of some mad routine or other. I was surprised to find nearly as much 'red tape' in France as in the Army at home : I never imagined it could follow one into the front line. True, some of it dropped off – one didn't salute – perhaps because there wasn't space – but it clung on where it could.

This red tape business is interesting and worth digression. It is a necessary evil in order to get some sort of efficiency out of inadequate people or institutions; just as conventions are necessary. But there is a longing in many of us to get away from it all – especially after the conventional and stifling surroundings of a public school followed by army routine. In a strange way the war had appealed to me as a means of getting away from everything I had ever known, away from all the pettiness of life into a world where death was so close that life must – surely – be lived naturally and at its best for sheer decency's sake. Yet for all I could see, the proximity of death, brought home as it had been by the annihilation of three-quarters of our officers and half our men a month before, made little difference to how people lived and thought. In fact the great thing was not to think and to stick hard to anything so tangible and comfortingly worldly as a bit of routine – for instance our full dress funeral of the man who drowned himself while bathing. I didn't understand : I was different. I was longing for a freedom which I could not explain, a freedom which probably comes only at death. I thought I should get it in battle – to keep. I got it and understood it but you can't keep it – it goes, dragged from you by all the pettiness of life and the strong red strings of our conventional ideas. In peace-time in ordinary society the most learned scientist is biased in his work by starting with a given attitude of mind : he has been brought up in a certain way with a certain set of ideas and these affect the way he approaches his work. I had an idea that war, or at least the stark reality of actual battle must dissolve all the mental veneer of conventional biases and leave one face to face with something real without a single frill, able to think clearly and act freely and to say this is right and that is wrong without any doubts. I was right up to a point. One had the vision but afterwards it was all just the same again – except perhaps that one was left a rebel, thinking differently from others on many things and never likely to see things again from the same viewpoint as those whom one would most wish to understand.

The story of 17th and 18th August must now proceed a stage. Later that night I was wandering aimlessly up and down the trench trying to get warm when I ran across Norton who was coming to look for someone to talk to. 'Let's go and look at — Company.' So I told Hogg I should be away for an hour or so and we worked our way up a narrow connecting trench which someone said led to the Company HQ. It was a lovely summer night, fresh and starry, but the air spoilt by that foul smell of gun cotton, that dirty smell of a burst shell. But it was quiet, the shelling was only desultory and there was not much in the way of fireworks along the front except some six miles to the north, 'Martinpush Way', where no one ever seemed to get any rest.

The Company HQ was a fine affair, a regular room, probably ten foot square, roofed with tin. It was not sunk and made no pretence of being shellproof but there was some earth on the tin which might have stopped a bullet if someone dropped some from overhead.

They were playing cards, an officer and a subaltern, but stopped when we came and asked if they knew what all this talk was about the rum. 'Rum ?' said Norton. 'Never heard of it and anyhow I don't like the sound of it, talk about something pleasanter.' I didn't know what he meant. Rum sounded inoffensive stuff to me – and anyhow Norton liked whisky – but certainly there was very obvious prejudice against this particular liquid in this Company HQ, so I changed the subject and asked if they would like to change quarters with us as Hogg was rather a large man for our small dug-out. For no apparent (to me) reason this produced an overflow of mirth.

'Captain bleedin' 'Ogg,' said someone and upset the packing case with the cards. Perhaps Hogg wasn't popular? But why – our veteran company commander?

Anyhow everyone was very friendly in the dug-out. Several rather senior subalterns whom I'd hardly dared to speak to (I was horribly 'junior') were there. There certainly was a difference in the front line and people who seemed of great importance back behind seemed to have shrunk, while some insignificant people seemed to be larger. Jack Rash, who was only a 2nd Lieutenant, seemed to be the chief personality there.

'So you've been having a tough time for a start off,' said Rash to me. 'There is some whisky there by the way if anyone wants it.' And people began to talk in a way that seemed so different from the officers' mess conversations at Halton. Everyone seemed more friendly and more natural in a queer way which I cannot describe. Artificialities disappear in close proximity to great danger – and I began to feel how pleasant people can be when they are themselves and not what they want other people to think of them. I was pondering what Rash's remark referred to. Someone else put in, 'Had you ever been on a working party before the other night?' 'No, why?' 'Half the company went, didn't they?' 'Yes.' 'What was it all about?' 'Well, I'm damned,' says someone else, 'sends a new subaltern on a job like that and sits at home himself – wants a good sleep I suppose – tired out poor devil.' 'Trying his bloody armour,' says another amidst loud applause. 'Steady now, remember Jerry's over there and likes a quiet night!' It now dawned on me for the first time to my great surprise that our Great Captain was regarded as a funk; secondly, that he wasn't popular, and thirdly, that I was.

At this moment an orderly entered with a message for the officer. The envelope bore the inscription in blue pencil, 'Secret and Confidential'. I noticed him change colour a bit as he initialled the envelope. He handed it to the orderly who departed and he then put the paper on the box in front of him and looked at Rash with a face like death. None of this had conveyed anything to me – orderlies and messages were common enough, though there certainly did seem something in the atmosphere. 'When?' said Rash. 'Dawn tomorrow.'

No one said much for a bit, then a voice, 'So the rum will be coming along perhaps.' 'Perhaps it's come; send along to Kenneth (that was Kenneth Turner, the Adjutant) and see if they've got it at Battalion HQ. We might get ours up and have a drop in the tea tonight if there's plenty.' 'Poor old you – first time up, and a first class show. What rotten luck,' said someone to me. 'I know someone who won't be there anyhow,' said the officer, 'and that's me. I can't stick it!' He had become quite white and his teeth looked as if they ought to be chattering. No one made any comment on his remark. If I had not seen his face I should not have believed he could be serious – a company officer. But more surprising still no one else appeared to be surprised or to have anything to say. At last someone said, 'Well, what can you do?' 'Go sick.' 'But the Old Man would never let an officer go sick and the aid post is in his dug-out – you can't get round Noble' (the doctor). 'Oh well, I've got a revolver,' said he and got up and went out into the trench. 'Bullet through his hand I suppose,' said someone pensively – 'Poor old devil he's whacked. Bravest boy in the battalion a few weeks ago.' 'What is he? About twenty-two?' 'He won't be here tomorrow night. I can see it in his face, he'd rather kill himself!' The most surprising thing to me was that no one criticised him, and he himself was quite open and unashamed. I had much to learn.[8]

The only other thing of interest to me that happened that night – 16th August – was an excursion along the front line trench. I went by myself to see the piece of trench occupied by our 'D' Company, who were on the right. I walked along the extreme right of their position and then beyond. Beyond their right-hand sentry post there was no one. The trench just went on. Presumably there should have been some sort of touch with the left company of the brigade and our right but there was not. I told the 'D' Company commander about this in a somewhat casual way – as it was no business of mine. He was however more interested in the whisky he was drinking and evidently indisposed to an excursion beyond his right flank. So I began to grope my way back to my own company feeling I had poked my nose sufficiently into other people's business.

To get back to the support trench there was a choice of CTs – one occupied by a Company HQ and another somewhat battered and disused. I used the latter. It was very dark and the trench quite deserted. In places it was broken entirely and most of the way the path was too irregular to go very fast. I remember quite suddenly being overcome with a sense of the loneliness of the place – an eerie feeling which I was to have again near High Wood two years later. I quickened my pace almost wanting to run to get away from the desolation of the place – with the obvious results: Another new experience but not an uncommon one. I scrambled to my feet repressing the urge to yell and blundered wildly down the trench in a panic of mingled terror and disgust.

There are various sorts of fear. I had now experienced one of them, the fear of disgustingly contorted dead bodies in lonely places. How good it was for me: I think I fancied myself rather a hero after the working party adventure the previous night. This was a sobering experience for me. Lots of public school boys aged seventeen to nineteen ought to fall over dead bodies in dark trenches; it would do them a power of good.

The remainder of the night was spent in spasmodic efforts to sleep sitting up in a niche in the side of the trench. News came to our company at some period that we were in for a show at dawn on the 18th: that we had to take the German front and support line trenches ahead of us while the 2nd Argyll on our left performed similarly in High Wood itself. The edge of the wood was our left boundary. This was what the talk of rum had been about at Company HQ and explained the officer's behaviour, though I doubt if I realised it just then.

On the next day[9] (unless I have got the dates wrong and all that I am relating was crowded into one night) our 'B' Company was moved to a trench further to the left behind our left company ('A'). I remember sitting in a trench for hours with shrapnel bursting overhead. For the Hun had got wind of the impending attack and was doing all he could to prevent massing of troops. We had a number of casualties. I remember talking to an officer of the Queen's who suddenly appeared. He spent the morning with our company and it appeared that he was to be assigned to the company whose HQ I had visited, and who going over the top the next morning. The officer I'd met had been evacuated as a casualty and we were so short of experienced officers that we had to apply for one from another regiment. He was an awfully nice fellow : I hope he got through – I never heard of him again so he was almost certainly killed.

The rest of this night I was very fully occupied. Orders came from Battalion HQ that our company were to dig a trench some thirty yards in front of the front line. This was called a 'jumping off' trench to be used for our first line of attack to start from, the hope being that the enemy barrage would come down beyond it. It had to be dug. There was of course no wire in front of our line as the line had only so recently been taken. Detailed orders came through. The trench was to start at the edge of High Wood at a point so many yards in front of our front line and to extend for some yards parallel to our front line. Touch was to be established with the HQ on the right company of the Argylls in the wood so that they should know what we were doing.

Hogg wasn't having any – not even measuring the ground or even looking at it. Robertson was to take two platoons and work for two hours or so; then I was to take the other two and finish it.

The history of this night was a nightmare of things going wrong. I was far too occupied to be in the least frightened : besides I had not had enough war yet to be frightened, provided I was not alone.

Robertson went off with his men. About one and a half hours later it seems that Battalion HQ became aware first that the trench had not been started and secondly that Robertson and all his men were lost. Hogg must have received a proper cursing for not seeing about the job himself for he went off to find his half-company, an ill considered piece of boldness which led to the cutting short of the overseas career of this veteran company commander. He set out like Achilles fully armed with his back piece of my body shield protecting his manly chest and stomach. But who can provide against the ill-timed jests of staff officers? This division of the brigade had ordered us to dig this trench. But so concerned were they to keep the secret from the Hun that they had even kept it from our own gunners who continued through the night to drop sundry shells short on my working party – to my extra annoyance.

So no sooner had the manly Hogg stepped from our front line

trench to seek his lost lambs, exposing his armoured frontage to the Hun, than a dexterous British gunner dropped one neatly behind him presenting him with a useful 'blighty' flesh wound. In the battalion aid post he insisted on being treated before a seriously wounded man and made the historic remark, 'They've got me at last.' He had been several weeks in France and was never seen in that country subsequently. I hope he is still a successful stockbroker.

The end of Hogg also saw the end of Robertson. I went to the Adjutant and told him that it was impossible to have the poor fellow getting in the way any longer and that he ought to be got rid of before the attack. It was not difficult to persuade Robertson himself to go to the MO and say he felt ill. Somehow he was spirited away to England where he stayed for the duration. When I saw him some years after the war he had taken to drink and his war experiences were in process of turning his brain – or rather his failure as he called it, poor chap.

Then I took my half-company to dig the neglected trench after finding Robertson's lost men and telling the CSM to look after them. But there wasn't much of the night left and the enemy lights were going up all the time so that between each shovelful one had to drop flat. I spaced the men out from the left, told them to dig a hole for themselves which they did quickly and then to connect their holes to their neighbours' – which they did slowly! I walked up and down encouraging or cursing them as seemed fit and taking a turn with a shovel here and there. We were lucky not to get sprayed by machine-guns and to have no actual casualties from our own shells. I wrote fruitless notes to Battalion HQ for transmission to the gunners but I expect the lines to Brigade had been cut and the runners were not likely to get through along 'Death Valley' that night. Brigade HQ were right back in Fricourt Wood and it was bad between them and us.

By the first suggestion of dawn we had a miserable series of holes completed and some of them joined up.

When I got back to my Company HQ I found myself the only officer in the company and therefore for the time I was in command of it. In due course Jack Rash was transferred to 'B' Company and we remained together until I became Adjutant some months (weeks perhaps only) late.[10]

The orders for the attack at dawn on 18th August involved 'A' and 'D' Companies going over together side by side with 'C' in support some fifty yards behind. My company, 'B' Company, was in 'reserve', a fact responsible for my being alive now. Our job was to go over with picks and shovels directly we saw 'A' and 'D' Companies jump into the German front line trench. Just before dawn 'A' and 'D' moved into the trenches we had recently dug and we moved up to the front line trench just behind 'A', 'C' being behind 'D'. During this movement the enemy opened an intense bombardment. It caught us in the CT between the support and the front line trenches. Even when there are no casualties a heavy bombardment produces a stupefying effect on men and they tend to become insensible to orders from sheer fear. I remember well my efforts to keep my half-company from getting into this dazed condition and incidentally to prevent them turning and making off whence they had come. We got wedged in a traffic jam for some minutes and it seemed touch and go whether they could be kept in a frame of mind to follow on. Especially was this so when the result of the jam became evident in the shape of strings of wounded coming down from further forward. Amongst these was young Suttle with all the fingers of one hand hanging by shreds of skin. He held up his hand as he passed me with a grimace but he knew this wound had saved his life. A few weeks later his photo appeared in the *Daily Mirror* with the inscription : 'This heroic young officer received seven wounds.'

This string of wounded men took the stuffing out of me a bit. Like most people I had not fully realised before that the horror of war is wounds, not death. I had thought of people being killed perhaps, if they weren't lucky enough to get a nice little wound first. I had never imagined, even remotely, what a man looks like with a wound in the stomach. Here for the first time I was brought up against the sickening horror of war. Not a case of fear now : I didn't think of myself being killed or wounded. I realised what war means for the first time and I suppose it is only experience that can make us realise it. I think my main feeling was of indignation – or am I imagining this as I write ? 'All this time I have been deceived into thinking war is heroic when really it is filthy and horrible beyond words. It is torture. Why can't we tell the people of England and Germany that these things are happening? They can't know or they would stop it all. We must tell them.' Thoughts like this and then a great thump in the back from a clod of earth to wake me up.

Soon we reached the front line just as 'A' and 'D' Companies left the jumping off trench. Then a crawl forward to the trench they had left. Shells falling so thick, such a racket, such a smoke, that one was hardly aware what was happening. Then I got my men spread out and warned to follow when I started to go forward in rushes, keeping in line if possible. Go. First rush, say, twenty yards, then flat. A few casualties. Then the unexpected. Just as I was about to start the next rush I looked up and there were the leading companies coming back or what was left of them. A struggling line of men running in a sort of staggering run. Some running, some dropping. The first few got level with me and as I looked at them I saw in their eyes that wild look of men mad with fear. All human qualities extinct and the look of the beast staring out through human eyes. I remember this so well and how I almost laughed as I thought how the heroic young officer in the storybook would shoot them with his revolver if they didn't turn back. You could shoot them but you couldn't turn them. They would go for miles like that till a shell stopped them or they fell senseless with exhaustion. Well, what was I to do? No good going on with picks and shovels. There was only my half-company left to withstand the most probable enemy counter-attack. 'A', 'D' and 'C' Companies were dissolved.

So I got my men digging like fury to consolidate a position. Just where were we? I didn't go back to the jumping off trench in case a few yards' retreat meant more and I failed to hold them. In half an hour or so when I got the order from Battalion HQ to consolidate to meet counter-attack it was satisfactory to be able to scrawl over the message, 'Have been doing so for some time.' It was of course the obvious thing to do but I think I got a lot of kudos for it and that it was a factor in bringing about my appointment as Adjutant later. Anyhow the Hun did not counter-attack and in an hour there was supreme peace all along the front.

In due course I ceased to be feverishly occupied: we had a

respectable trench connected into the old front line. I decided to wander off to look for Norton and my other friends. Even then I had not imagined them being killed. But as I progressed along the old front line and asked the stray men, who seemed to be scattered pointlessly about, if they had seen Mr So and So, it suddenly came to me that they might – must have been killed. The men I asked looked as if they had never heard of Mr Norton or Mr Bedwell or Mr Pawsey.[11] They looked at me as if I was asking about people who had lived a very long time ago.

The next shock of war had come to me – the next experience – the death of one's friends. It didn't seem possible. I jumped out of the trench and ran forward into no-man's land. 'We must find them, perhaps they are lying here wounded' : just that one thought. Answered by 'phut, phut, phut', as an enemy machine-gun spattered the ground at my feet. 'Come back, sir, you can't do any good,' from an old man in the trench behind. I came back. Wounded they might be but there they must lie till they died, for no living man could go to their help – certainly not the only officer but two left in the battalion – just the Colonel, Jack Rash and I – all the rest had gone, even the doctor. I got back into the trench and cried till I couldn't see.

In half an hour or so everything was quiet except that German machine-guns opened fire at once if anyone showed above ground. A few of our stretcher bearers were able to crawl out from shell hole to shell hole giving first-aid to anyone wounded who was still alive and hadn't been able to crawl in. But this only applied within twenty yards of our trench and even so the risk was very great and it was impossible to drag men in. Beyond this distance the bulk of our wounded must have been and nothing was ever done for them. It was almost as dangerous after dark and also almost impossible to find people.

I spent some time crawling about locating wounded and pointing them out to stretcher bearers. One of these bearers had been working increasingly at getting people in who were near enough to drag and now he was working further afield crawling about with bandages and iodine and a water-bottle. The look in his eyes was such a contrast with what I had seen earlier in the eyes of those men who were running away. It was also a contrast with the dull expression of the people who were left. It is scarcely an exaggeration to say that the soul of this man seemed to be shining through his eyes as he went about his dangerous work of mercy. His face was beautiful. If one has seen such an expression on a human face it takes more than the ordinary arguments of clever agnostics to persuade one that there is no God. Though it is true that many to whom the war gave certain experiences which they can never describe or share have little use for the prescribed ways of worshipping that God. The face of that man is still quite vivid in my memory and that light in his eyes. It has a very great significance for me.

Editor : With the exception that the date of the relief was two days earlier than he remembered it, and that it was 'C' Company, not 'A' Company, who were alongside his own 'B' Company, the facts of his narrative are borne out by official documents. The only 'opinion' expressed in the war diary was that in the attack on the 18th : 'The new drafts conducted themselves admirably.'

Stormont Gibbs : At this point the curtain falls and I remember nothing until the morning of probably the next day but two, when we were in camp well back, drafting into the remains of our companies large batches of recruits, officers and men, mostly straight from England.

So I propose before proceeding further to digress – first for the purpose of telling from after knowledge the story of what actually took place when our attack failed.

It appears that the Germans put into practice a recently devised plan according to which, when an enemy attack was anticipated, they send out snipers to lie in shell holes well out in no-man's land. These snipers would be far enough out to be within or nearly within our creeping barrage, and would take up their positions during the night. Very brave men – probably volunteers for the job. As we go over the top the snipers pick off each officer as soon as he comes within certain range. This appears to have happened in almost every case. It was said, however, that Pawsey went on with a bullet through his neck and actually reached the German trench before collapsing: that Bedwell also reached the German line and took his men into it before he was killed and his men driven out by counter-attack. Bedwell had just left a public school sixth form and carried the *Iliad* about with him. What a magnificent type of man compared with the officers we got later from secondary schools or from the ranks. Nor was he the only example of the superiority of the public school boy – and of the public school boys the quiet scholarly type were the best. The smart young men and the athletes would throw their weight about behind the lines but they were not chosen for a nasty job and after a few months' real war they were likely to crack up. The middle-aged married men and the quiet young men were the war's heroes – and how much harder it was for them too.

There is no doubt in my mind that the best of England's men were killed in the war. The ex-officer one knows twenty years later is often the braggart type – who may even think of the 'good old war days' – and the public do not realise that the survivors were not the heroes as a rule. A certain type of man managed to get into something that wasn't the Infantry anyhow – nor yet the Field Artillery. There were as many safe jobs as dangerous ones comparatively speaking. And there are living today very, very few men who led their platoons over the top, for instance, more than once. These men are so few in fact that they could have no influence whatever in spreading a real view of war – unless they happen to be writers of sufficient merit to make their books attractive reading. Mr Churchill once said – though I can hardly think he is accurate – that for every man in the army who *really* fought there were six who didn't. It depends of course what you mean by fighting. Personally I have never met a man who has pushed a bayonet into someone's stomach. I suppose this is a perfectly possible operation for a disciplined guardsman, a wild Australian, a drunken Englishman. But I have never seen it done and I couldn't do it myself to save a kingdom. Even the Archbishops could not persuade me that such a thing could be my duty.

It is not the purpose of this narrative to make out a good case for my regiment, though I loved it more than any other corporate institution of which I have ever been a member[12] for it was human. The regiment did well that 18th August though they scarcely took and never retained any objective. There was much mismanagement and I am fairly sure no responsible member of the staff knew the ground about which he was issuing orders. Our brigadier and brigade major were splendid people but the divisional staff were probably unintelligent and certainly inefficient.

Editor : Contrary to the myth the 'High Command', i.e. the senior generals, were not hated by the troops, a lot of regimental officers were loved, but 'the Staff' were generally held (often quite unfairly) in universal contempt and hated by the entire Army. Again Siegfried Sassoon :

> 'Good-Morning; Good-Morning,' the General said
> When we met him last week on our way to the line
> Now the soldiers he smiled at are most of 'em dead,
> And we're cursing his staff for incompetent swine.
> 'He's a cheery old card', grunted Harry to Jack
> As they slogged up to Arras with rifle and pack.
>
> — — — —
>
> But he did for them both by his plan of attack.

Stormont Gibbs : It seems to me hardly credible anyhow for Suffolk yokels to get as far an objective with at most two officers – who were probably both wounded. It also seems fairly obvious that with no officers they would not remain in a highly dangerous and uncomfortable place. It may be suggested that the sergeants and other NCOs should have held the men together. But the suggestion would not come from anyone aware of the ineffectiveness of the average NCO under shell fire. There are exceptions – and then they ought to be officers. This may only apply in the infantry where promotion is so rapid owing to continual casualties. It could apply to our 'regulars'. Our high-class parade-ground company sergeant-major, an old regular soldier, could not be taken into the line or he inspired panic. [This sort of NCO was vividly described in Robert Graves' 'Sergeant-Major Money'.]

And now to proceed with the narrative. After a few days' rest our companies, which had emerged about a third of strength, had been made up with further supplies of 'cannon fodder'. Our brigade returned to the line on the immediate right of our previous position.

Two battalions would have been in the line, the left one being just right of where we had been before, the right one having Delville Wood on its right flank. Our battalion went into support trenches on the high ground in front of Mametz village. We overlooked High Wood and the ridge joining it to Delville Wood where we had recently had our battle. From our position we had a splendid view of a large sector of the Somme front and the fireworks at night all round were very beautiful.

Fireworks are no longer beautiful to me and the smell of them recalls scenes I prefer to forget. But each November I watch them and I sometimes wonder if I should be compelled to do so if people knew the curious sensations they invoke.

Now followed another period in the front line which in some ways was more unpleasant than the last. It provided a different series of experiences – to such an extent that when it was over I had the feeling that I was really an old soldier and for that matter I was – I was the oldest soldier but six in the battalion, speaking only of combatant officers. It is very true that a day could be a year in the war in the intensity and variety of experience it might bring.

This new period in the line was ushered in by a working party on the previous night as before. As I was the only officer who had been in the line before apart from Jack Rash and the new company commanders I was the obvious person to do it. Again we had to dig a trench in a position to be indicated by a guide to be met at a certain spot. Again that trench was never dug.

Now I had begun to be frightened and the thought of taking half a company all by myself over that awful ground was too much. I felt sure I should lose my men and actually of course the trouble was, what if I had casualties? I had seen casualties since my last working party and I was terrified of not being able to dispose of wounded men suitably, for the party would only take two stretcher bearers.

When Jack Rash told me I was to take the party he explained what I had to take in the way of tools, etc., and all the time I got more and more glum. Finally, I murmured, 'I wish you were coming too.' Well, there were only two of us in the company, so how could he? For it would mean no one left with those who weren't going. But Rash offered to go instead. It was not his job and what other

49

company commander would have made that offer? I couldn't have that, of course – in fact I had already been a bit poor in admitting my funk of going alone. In the end it was suggested to the Adjutant that it was a job for two officers – and as far as that goes it most certainly was, but there was such a shortage. So leave was given for us both to go. That I always remained very devoted to Jack Rash is not to be wondered at. Then it came to moving off. Rash was to lead and I to go at the back of the long string of men as they moved slowly along a battered CT known as Orchard Street. Again I murmured gently, 'Can't I come with you?' and I did. He led and I went second, a corporal and two stretcher bearers in the rear. I suppose the column was forty yards long.

Orchard Street connected the trenches of the battalion in support with the support trenches just behind in the front line, perhaps half a mile or three-quarters of a mile ahead. But the front was very irregular, for the brigade on the right had recently driven the enemy out of Delville Wood (New Zealanders) whilst the attack on the left had failed. So we had a front line trench in the air in front of Delville Wood actually in advance of the actual German front line on the left. Our support trench was in fact the old German front line and the Germans were in it a hundred yards on our left with the sandbag partitions erected by both sides. Thus Orchard Street ran up to the old German front line which was now our support trench and occupied by the 2nd Argyll. In front of them were either the King's Liverpools or the 4th Middlesex in the front line trench in the air. Orchard Street joined this old German trench at the NW corner of Delville Wood. The trench was called Wood Lane.

There is something very stirring about a place name. The names of French villages which I have entirely forgotten, but at which we fought or rested in hovels, have the same curious effect on me now as the first sight of the coast of Kent from the 'Leave Boat' used to have. And the trench names are something the same. But of all trench names Orchard Street and Wood Lane stand out as symbolic of frightfulness. I can never mention a walk along these roads in London without a vision of Delville Wood before my eyes. The words themselves are pleasant sounds – wood, orchard, lane, but when written or spoken as street names they are to me the most sinister and monstrous expressions in the language. (I cannot expect of course that if anyone ever reads this they will not think it absurd.)

So we started along Orchard Street bound for Wood Lane. Orchard Street was so narrow that a very fat man would have stuck. It was normally about six feet deep but about a quarter of the distance on an average it became about one foot deep or even lost itself owing to having been crushed in by a large shell. The valley through which it was wound was very heavily shelled, in fact it consisted merely of continuous shell holes. Our progress was slow for the shelling was persistent. In some places a series of scurries and crouchings. Some of the heavy stuff had that particular businesslike tone that meant it was coming as near as nothing on top of you. Shells would fall right by the trench or in it just ahead round the corner leaving one deaf and stunned. Men next door to each other had to shout to be intelligible above the din. At one point we had to wait a quarter of an hour because the shells were falling so thick in the trench just ahead. During this wait the ominous cry of 'stretcher bearers' was passed up. It originated in the middle and was passed both ways. Nothing could be done as there was not room to pass anyone in this trench. Rash merely passed down the order that stretcher bearers were not to leave the party without permission. It seems that two men had been partially buried and one slightly wounded in the arm. So the stretcher bearers weren't needed after all.

It was very dark and soon we lost our way for the trench vanished for some distance. I was beginning now, in face of necessity and the general state of chaos, to get back a certain amount of nerve. So I went ahead to explore. I ran across some irregular ground in what seemed the right direction, saw a hole ahead and jumped. As I did so a ghastly figure loomed ahead in the light of a bursting shell stretching out its arms to receive me. I probably yelled but there was no one to hear. I landed in the Delville Wood boundary ditch and was crouching against a stunted rooty hedge. When I found I had not been caught by a goblin or the Kaiser I had a look round. Through the hedge was Delville Wood, dark and forbidding. The light of explosions and I think a certain amount of moon now showed that there was not a living tree or shrub – all was short and blackened. The ditch was evidently meant for a trench and Orchard Street was meant to run into it. So I rediscovered the rest and brought them on. Rash was just behind me and we proceeded along the ditch slowly. It was certainly lighter now and we came to a point where the ditch widened out into a piece of low ground several feet wide with a tree on the left and the hedge on the right. Here evidently another trench was joined in from the left round the tree – Wood Lane.

I went on a few yards to the tree and there came upon a tragedy. Two Scotsmen lying in blood with both legs of each severed between hip and knee. They were not really unconscious. One was feebly moaning 'stretcher bearers' over and over again and writhing the upper part of his body about. The other as I stooped over them said, 'Shoot me you —' I ran back to Rash and said, 'Get the stretcher bearers quick and come and look at these men.' He came and told me that it was not our business; we should probably need our own SB's ourselves, whilst if they went off with these men they would be away for the rest of the night; further, the men could not live. 'Well, we're not allowed to carry morphia,' I said. 'And we must do something.' And my hand went to my revolver. 'You must not do that,' he said – and we stepped over the men and they cursed us.

All our half-company stepped over those dying men who lay in their way and left them as they were. These things have to be. There was nothing we could do for them but shoot them and this was not allowed. For in war-time all the decencies of civilisation, all moral codes which interfere with killing the enemy are suspended. But those laws which if suspended too would ease human sufferings are retained in all their rigour. Even in war 'Thou shalt not murder'. I have always considered myself a coward for not shooting those men and damn the consequences. I can feel great sympathy for the man who murders his wife and his children when the economic conditions of our 'civilisation' have made life intolerable for the family. When it is a case of killing a man who must otherwise die in agony there seems no two ways about it – in war-time; though it seems there are sound arm-chair arguments against it in peace-time.[13] When we returned four hours later the men were still there – alive – but I trust unconscious.

After another twenty yards or so of progress there was a light ahead. A dive down a few steps and we found ourselves, Rash and I, in the Company HQ of the support company of the battalion of the line – the 2nd Argylls. A wooden table with a candle that jumped as the shells exploded around the place. A company commander and a few subalterns. We said who we were and that we had just passed two of their men badly wounded – full description. They were not very interested and did nothing whatever about it. Such is the callousness of war. I was horrified. But of course there is, when you come to think of it, no point in risking the lives of sound men carrying dying men from one place to another. We asked for instructions as to where we had to go and dig. They didn't know and didn't care much as long as they didn't have to emerge from their fairly secure hole. A very proper attitude. 'But,' said the OC Company, 'who the — sent you poor — up here anyway? How can any mortal dig anything up here on a night like this? Someone at Division wants to be able to put in a pretty-looking trench on his map, I suppose.' 'Our orders are to meet a guide on the left of the front line trench.' 'What! You can't go there! No one can, let alone a working party of fifty men!' 'That's our orders.'

It was raining now – moisture as well as everything else. We rejoined our men and supposed we must go on – for a bit anyhow – in the expectation of meeting a guide. The officers of this company of 'Jocks' could only indicate our direction and declare that the whole neighbourhood was an unsuitable habitation for man.

We advanced along Wood Lane for perhaps a few hundred yards. It was quite deserted. I have no idea where the men of the Argyll Company were – in the wood behind us, I suppose. Then suddenly we came upon a couple of men who stopped us, talking in a loud Scottish whisper. 'You can't go on. They get everyone.' The situation was certainly unpleasant. Just ahead was a pile of sandbags blocking the trench. A way round them was scooped out making it possible to go on beyond but at intervals a bullet would strike them on the other side. The Germans we were told were in the trench some thirty yards further up. It was straight and they kept firing down it. To get to the front line one had to proceed another short distance and then turn right. The thing was impossible without certain casualties and the possibility of machine-guns making a complete massacre.

Already there were wounded men lying between the sandbags crying for water. The only other means of progress would be to run over the top in the probable direction of the front line. We agreed this would be absurd; there was too much wire and too many lights going up. We decided to wait for a bit in case a guide got through. And then I suddenly forgot everything for the next two days except the isolated act of stepping over the wounded men on the return journey – no digging having been accomplished.

In a couple of days it was our turn to relieve the 2nd Argylls in the front line. Rash and I knew the ropes so it was decided we should relieve the front line company. Only one company was in the front line – in the air – quite cut off by day and usually by night too. One company was in support with HQ at the dug-out where we found the Argyll officers on the working party night. Battalion HQ and two companies were right back in reserve at the end of Orchard Street – perhaps a mile back near the support battalion. An unusual arrangement but probably a good one – a depth arrangement with three companies available for counter-attack if, as was possible, the front company (that's us) were annihilated or lost. We were to be in this front line trench for forty-eight hours. It was, I think, before the days of iron rations, anyhow we had none. We had a meal at supper time and the 'relief' started a little before midnight. Rations would be sent up to us by a party before dawn, when the relief was completed. (None came, of course.)

During a relief there is a period when double strength is in the line, the incomers and the outgoers. It is a fine moment for the enemy to bombard if he knows there is a relief in progress. Apparently he did.

Our company led, by the same route as before – Orchard Street. 'A' Company followed to go into support. We moved up without incident and in comparative quiet until we reached the sandbag barrier. A sort of shallow trench had been constructed now to make it possible to reach the front line without exposure to direct fire. It was about 4 ft 6 ins deep at its best. We were mostly packed into this when there was a jam in front owing to a downcoming stretcher – it appeared – but I didn't know the cause at the time for I was in the middle. No one moved for what seemed hours and nothing could be done, for you couldn't get past anyone or over the top and messages passed up merely lost themselves as was so often the case. But there was more to it (now I remember))than a stretcher party. There was a length of trench which had been blown in the previous day burying half a dozen men. The process of crossing this was exceedingly slow.

At this point I must have gone wrong in the story for, though I know it was a moonlight night for the relief, I do not think aeroplanes did night flying at that stage. Either they must have done or else dawn must have come to us before completion – I can't remember which but almost certainly the latter. What I do remember vividly is that while packed in this little CT like sardines a German plane flew low up and down overhead. I remember the feverish efforts to prevent the men looking up and the momentary expectation of an annihilating bombardment. I forget the rest of the relief process except for the delight of the outgoers at being relieved before the supposedly inevitable attack – which would have been quite irresistible; no wire, no one on the right flank as far as could be discovered and the enemy certainly on the left flank in the same trench and in another trench a hundred yards ahead. Delville Wood gaunt and lonely behind – some fifty yards behind with wire in between – for this was an old German trench we were in.

It was an odd trench, this nameless outpost of the 33rd Division. Actually, no one knew just where it was or rather which bits we were in and which bits the Hun. The divisional staff naturally wanted to be precise about it to direct our artillery suitably; so we were given flares to take up to light when our aeroplane came over. Early in the day it came. It has to say QCM. That meant, 'Light your flares, you blighters, before they shoot me down.' QCM on a klaxon goes er-er-e-er-er-e-er-e, er, er, er er. The poor thing flew up and down for half an hour coming lower and lower emitting those agonising cries amidst shrapnel and bullets. All our flares were damp!

So we remained isolated and unknown with our own artillery as liable to murder us as to help us. Half-way along this line was Company HQ – a nook out about three feet square with a bit of tin across the top. Opposite was another nook in which the CSM sat with his teeth chattering with terror : the poor man trembled for forty-eight hours, and was as useless as jelly. We never took him into the line again. The trench was one of those ones where there really were boots projecting themselves as if offering to be cleaned, shiny scalps and noses of half-buried bodies that one walked on – in fact bits about the place generally. Worse, perhaps, there were many dead bodies in front and behind the trench near the parapet. Several had been shot in the stomach and their insides were ballooning out and swarming with bluebottles. It was a hot August. The place stank. It was a veritable hell.

One of us remained at Company HQ while the other patrolled the line. We had no food or water for forty-eight hours, i.e. until after we were relieved. When I felt faint from undernourishment, as I did once or twice, I found I could live on whisky, of which I had about a quarter of a pint.

One of the first duties after a relief was to make contact with the people on one's flanks. It would usually have been helpful to be told before a relief who these people were. But usually this did not happen. We knew the only people on our left were the enemy. We had no idea who, if anyone, was on our right. Fruitless efforts were made to find someone. We felt horribly isolated; flanks in the air and no communication with the rear possible by day. By night it took several hours to send a message back to Battalion HQ and receive a reply. One communication in the course of a night might be possible and this consisted of, 'Send water and food. Can't we have a machine-gun?' No reply.

Two events of interest took place the day after the relief. I had gone along to the extreme left of the line shortly after what would have been breakfast time. There had been a casualty from shell fire and a man named Self, a tailor in private life, was lying dead in the trench. A man nearby was cleaning his buttons and another cleaning boots. These occupations were symptoms of a mixture of boredom and apprehension on the part of the very 'Suffolk' men concerned. It would have been more appropriate if the men concerned had been playing at soldiers; for just beyond the neat traverse along the trench came the sound of an exploding bomb. The men were entirely uninterested imagining it was merely a small shell and, 'What could they do about it!'

I went on a few yards to the traverse and scrambled into a position where I could see over thirty yards away was the large sandbag wall marking the finish of the German position. Leaning over this wall was a German with his rifle aimed at my head. From behind him came a bomb thrown by one of his friends and landing a good way short of my traverse. Evidently the Germans were to make an effort to recapture their old trench (in which we now were) by flank bombing attacks down the trench.

A bullet passed near my head and I realised we were in for something serious. I remember that the man behind me continued to clean his boots. It seemed like a nightmare : he took no interest at all, and anyhow what was the good, for we had no bombs? If nothing could be done, there was no particular reason why the Hun should not drive us out of the trench with very great ease.

This was an occasion when I was rather cool-headed though scared stiff. I ducked, examined my revolver which was fully loaded and found I had another dozen bullets in a pouch. After thinking out a plan and realising that it was to be a case of rifle v. revolver. I bobbed up and fired. He fired simultaneously but a shade high. This process continued at a few seconds' interval, my rival firing higher and higher and my bullets went by his head as he came up. For his party to proceed down the trench (there was no traverse between him and me) it was necessary for him to remain up and cover his friends by keeping me down. Though if they had made a rush I couldn't have gone on shooting them for long. I thought they would, but doubtless they pictured the British Army behind me and not just a Suffolk ploughboy cleaning his boots.

During these tense seconds two nightmares ran through my head. (1) What when I emptied the chamber of my revolver – I should have to get down to reload? Then he would be up and they would rush. My fingers would go numb and refuse to reload without fumbling and dropping everything. (2) What if I shot the man? What would his mother feel like? I'd never killed a man and I hoped I should miss him but scare him. This was the nature of a prayer – a most urgent agonising one – and the end of the incident was tame, like most answers to prayer – effective, tame and (after the event) the obvious solution. My sixth and last shot went pretty close for I was quite good with a revolver. His shot went very high. He never bobbed up again and not another bomb was thrown.

After this alarm was over I began to go panicky. I went along to Rash at Company HQ and asked him to swap places a bit as someone seemed necessary on the left extremity and for the time being I daren't go back there. So he went.

It then became my business to keep a watch ahead. We had an unpleasant feeling that the Hun meant to recapture this trench somehow and having failed in his flank attack he might well try a frontal affair. I don't know whether it was merely due to jumps but soon I thought I could see movement like men crawling a hundred yards or more ahead. The ground was very rough and pitted and there was plenty of cover beyond a distance of fifty yards for men to crawl along more or less unobserved. Anyhow we had no machine-guns and for the most part the firing step was on the wrong side of the trench (we had no shovels) so the general quietness on our part was most inviting to the enemy. In fact they may have wondered where our line actually was.

Soon I became convinced that men were crawling and I expected them any moment to get up and charge at our trench; I knew they could do so without losing more than a quarter of their number in the process.

Now we had one very precious possession – only one and whichever of us happened to be at HQ carried it carefully about with him – an SOS rocket. We had looked at it doubtfully many times wondering if it was dry. The purpose of an SOS rocket is to inform the gunners that one is being attacked and will they please put down a heavy barrage on no-man's land and the enemy trenches immediately. Now in our case it was quite uncertain if our gunners knew where we were and they might equally have put their barrage on us as on the enemy. Further, there was no other sort of rocket for saying 'Shut up' if they did go wrong. Further still, we had only the rocket and could only ask for artillery support once therefore. It was a very precious possession that I had in my hand, looking like a schoolboy straight from Hamleys.

Now I became convinced about the crawling men, though now, years after, I tend to believe they did not exist. The responsibility of popping off the rocket wanted sharing : I sent word for Rash to come and meet me at the HQ as quick as possible if he could leave the left flank. 'How do you fire a rocket, CSM?' I hadn't the vaguest idea: my father had always seen to this part on Guy Fawkes days. CSM said you needed something to put the stick in but he was quite unhopeful about finding anything.

Then Rash arrived. He agreed that they were probably crawling men and was for popping it off. 'You do it.' 'No, you!' Just then there was a bang on the left flank. Rash rushed back to his post with the parting words, 'Blow it off.' I crouched in the trench with the end of the stick on the ground and coming up between my thighs. Then I lit up. There was the usual rocket sound but instead of the usual spectacle there was disaster. The thing was badly aimed; it rose a few feet and then dived with great velocity, shooting along, fizzing parallel with the ground and finally descended approximately in the German front line. Some said figures were seen to rise and scamper from its flaming path; others that the enemy, seeing Apollo in his flaming chariot coming after them so venomously, decided to await a more propitious moment. But these things were said later in officers' messes where the thing became a stock joke – which I came to regard as feeble. The plain result of my badly aimed rocket was that the artillery did not open because they did not see it, the enemy did not attack because they probably never intended to, we had a perfectly quiet night without having to think of keeping the rocket dry because we hadn't one.

We were relieved without incident. My memory goes blank for a period which may have been a fortnight. But one very tragic event must here be recorded. Our casualties in the front line were negligible though we had had plenty of alarms and great discomfort. 'A' Company in support fared worse. For the Hun could safely bombard the support line without fear of hitting his own men. 'A' Company HQ to which I have already referred was a dug-out in the sense that it had a roof perhaps with some inches of soil on top. Captain Glanville had 'A' Company, a charming oldish man who had just come out – probably for the second time – a quiet kindly man. I forget his subalterns but I believe all were in the HQ together when it happened. They received a direct hit from a heavy shell and were all buried in it. One likes to think they were also killed by the shell.[14] For one of the worst horrors of the war was the possibility of being buried alive – or semi-alive – it not infrequently happened.

I have since discovered the position of this 'A' Company tomb – some fifteen years later. As you walk east up the north side of the now young and smiling wood there is an angle, a sharp right turn and then after twenty yards a left turn again. At the first angle just inside the hedge, undisturbed, unmarked and unknown (perhaps to anyone but me), are the remains of this old dug-out overgrown with nettles and thick brambles. It is only recognisable by the fact that the ground sinks like an irregular shell hole.[15] In contrast on the hill to the left stands the magnificent New Zealand memorial. There is no memorial to Captain Glanville or to any of 'A' Company of the 4th Suffolk. Their names may appear in the regimental war diary as having been casualties at a given date. There may be more alive who know just what happened to them.

There is a further contrast if you visit Delville Wood today. The village of Longueval – another terrifying word to me – has been rebuilt in red brick. An *estaminet* keeps a supply of the foulest Guinness for the benefit of English tourists. If you go as I did, a pilgrim to sacred ground, you should avoid the *estaminet*. It probably contains English tourists exhibiting their best party manners to the natives. Nauseating.

The Somme Today

Editor: The Somme battlefield has today (1986) reverted very much to its pre-Great War condition – a sleepy and very beautiful agricultural backwater.

At a first glance it is difficult to imagine the total devastation[16] it suffered in that summer of 1916. Lush green, ripening corn, mature woods (nearly all re-grown on the exact locations of their predecessors) rolling downland, the tumbling waters of the little Ancre alive with trout; all would lead the casual and uninformed visitor to think that here was a hiker's and fisherman's paradise. Blissfully he would be unaware that once it was more terrible than hell itself.

However, one does not have to look far to be reminded that something incredible did happen here – it is virtually impossible to find a spot from where one cannot see a cross of sacrifice brooding over a war cemetery – memorials abound, and one only has to scratch the surface (quite literally) to reap what is known as the 'Iron Harvest' of war.

The British alone fired over twenty-five million shells during the battle and the ground is impregnated with metal. (A third of these shells did not explode, and this was partly responsible for the great 'Munitions Scandal' which in turn had much to do with the replacement of Asquith by Lloyd-George as Prime Minister.)

In a thunderstorm the lightning flickers and cracks across the very face of the earth and a geiger counter simply goes berserk. A wander across a ploughed field can result in the walker picking up more bits of shrapnel, shrapnel balls, etc., than he can carry in his hands. One can easily walk in a single day at a leisurely pace from place to place, the route taken by the 4th Suffolk in those two months.

Indeed when the peasant farmers returned to their devastated home lands after the war they initially derived their income, whilst returning the land to an arable condition, by selling vast quantities of lead and brass[17] recovered from the battlefield.[18] It is still a very dangerous place, and each year both cattle and humans suffer injury by detonating unexploded ammunition of all types.[19]

NOTES

[1] There were in fact eight new 2nd lieutenants including C.P. (C. P. Parry-Crooke whom he had been at Radley with and who was to be his lifelong friend) and 283 other ranks. Geoffrey Adams (also at Radley with them) came out in September and was killed on 1st November.

[2] Here his memory is very wrong. The captain rejoined the battalion in France in September 1916 and remained with it till the end of the war.

[3] H. C. Pawsey actually also came out in the same draft.

[4] 2nd Lieutenant H. C. Pawsey is buried in Caterpillar Valley Cemetery, Longueval.

[5] In fact the battalion moved up on the evening of Sunday, 6th August, to relieve 4th Battalion Seaforth Highlanders, Church Parade having been held in the morning.

[6] 1930. Still today in 1986 it is not difficult to find ample evidence of battle.

[7] C.T. – Communication Trench.

[8] He had already won the Military Cross. His is a typical story of a brave man who never the less had come to the end of that limited reservoir of courage given to most men. Today shellshock and other conditions of sheer battleweariness are much better understood than they were then. He later returned to the battalion and was wounded.

[9] Yes, it was the next day.

[10] 1st January 1917.

11 2nd Lieutenant V. L. S. Bedwell has no known grave and is commemorated on the Thiépval Memorial. 2nd Lieutenant E. Norton is buried close to 2nd Lieutenant H. C. Pawsey in Caterpillar Valley Cemetery, Longueval.

12 He also loved Gayhurst School, but this was written in 1930.

13 I often wonder whether in fact Gibbs could have pulled the trigger. I well remember an occasion in 1952 when together we discovered a badly wounded bird in his garden at Bourne End. That it needed putting out of its misery he did not doubt, but left it to me, a twelve year old boy, to do, while he himself turned his back.

14 They weren't – Captain B. St. J. Glanville was dug out and subsequently died of his wounds. He is buried in Dantzig Alley Cemetery, Mametz.

15 Again, another fifty years on, I was able to find the exact spot from these directions, but only from knowledge of this narrative did I know that this was not just another shell hole.

16 I have always been surprised, having read so many contemporary accounts at how few actual veterans of the battle to whom I have spoken mentioned the mud. I personally think this is because they were also to experience Passchendaele the following year. One, however, did say that in the Ancre Valley it was even worse than Flanders.

17 A British body handed over to the authorities for decent burial was worth five shillings.

18 Approximately one hundred tons of unexploded material are still unearthed and then destroyed by the French and Belgian Armies each year on the British Sector of the Western Front alone.

19 The French government had intended, as at Verdun, to turn the area into a forest, it being considered impossible for it to revert to conventional agricultural land. The area was, however, under British military control and the British authorities did not feel it was their business to deny the peasants access to their own homelands once the fighting was over. Many lost their lives in the early years in the work of restoration.

CHAPTER THREE

Winter

Stormont Gibbs : The 4th Suffolk left the Somme battlefield at the beginning of September 1916. They had entered it in July and in those two months had suffered very heavily. The draft of officers who went out from home just before me had disappeared, mostly killed before I arrived at the end of July. Of the officers who were there when I arrived only the CO and Rash remained of the front line officers. Those who remained at transport lines were still the same : The second-in-command, transport officer and QM. Other ranks would not of course have suffered so heavily in proportion but certainly over half the battalion would have to be replaced by fresh recruits.

On leaving the Somme we were put into a quiet piece of line a few miles north of Hebuterne. I remember the amazing contrast – for I had not yet seen an ordinary piece of line where there had been no battle. Only a mile or two back we slept in a fairly complete little village the night before going into trenches. I particularly remember the birds were singing in the trees and the sight of the green grass and green leaves which we had not seen for weeks.

It was at this village that I had the great disappointment of being withdrawn from my company and separated from Rash whom I liked.[1] Our adjutant had been wounded at High Wood and for the time being a staff officer was borrowed to take his place, Fison. But this was only a temporary arrangement and so it was decided to try me out for the job. I don't quite know why and I have never since asked the CO. I have always imagined that he thought I had been clever when I made the necessary preparations to meet the counter-attack at High Wood before getting orders from him to do so. Also

I had not yet begun to show signs of fear : I was too much a public school boy still to dare to be frightened.

Anyhow Fison handed over to me an orderly room complete with a sergeant, beloved Sergeant Roe, a corporal, Corporal Herring (known as 'Muchly', which appears to be Hindustani for that fish) and two more clerks; several trunks full of papers and records and a typewriter.

I was then initiated into the mysteries of the 'office work' which runs a battalion. A war-time adjutant is seldom concerned with ceremonial drills and the normal routine work of the peace-time orderly room. He is in the unfortunate position of being a front line officer when the battalion is in the trenches or rather 'in the line' and of finding when he comes out of the line and back to his clerks and his typewriter an accumulation of correspondence and routine office stuff which allows him no rest until it is time to go in the line again. He has to be prepared to be woken at all times of the night to talk on the telephone or write or receive orders and in fact he cannot expect anything but an alternation of front line and hard work with no relaxing of any sort. His 'office' may be a hut, a dug-out, or an open field or trench. All his office gear has got to be kept mobile and is being moved from place to place every few days. What a job! The pay is fairly good, some twenty-five shillings a day, if I remember rightly, as captain and adjutant, and nothing to spend it on. But in war when you are unlikely to emerge alive your pay seems a thing of very little consequence. Actually I don't think I was aware what my pay did amount to until the war was over and I went to see what had accumulated in Cox's – some £300 I think apart from a large gratuity.

Well, there we were at Hebuterne and I remember the peace of the grass-grown trenches and the fact that we had only one casualty in the three days or more we were in the line.

After Hebuterne my memory deserts me for two to three months. I have recollections of sundry huts and dug-outs and an occasional billet, of a trek to another part of the line and back again, of cold nights in the snow[2] (or was that the next year?) until we finally got back to the Somme battle area sometime in mid-winter and fetched up at Clery-sur-Somme.

Editor : This period of late 1916 and early 1917 was for the battalion a relatively quiet one, and very typical of the life lived by infantry battalions when not engaged in pitched battles.

Short periods spent in 'quiet' parts of the line ('cushy trenches' in Tommies' slang) were supplemented by periods of rest behind the lines. But rest really meant a succession of parades and training – it was not the policy of the higher command to give the men much time for idleness and thinking. Time in support of the front line could often be the worst of all: supplying non-stop working parties for carrying forward the seemingly inexhaustible sinews of war, and digging and improving the trench system.

Casualties were relatively light – in September, for instance, the Suffolks lost one man killed and nine wounded, whereas the previous month they lost sixty-four killed (including three officers), ninety-nine wounded (ten officers) and forty-eight missing.

But there were raids mounted and repulsed and, because of their relative smallness compared to full scale battle, these were often remembered by the participants and onlookers with more clarity than the storm of total conflict.

During this period the 33rd Division acquired a new commandant, Major-General R. J. Pinney, and the brigade a new brigadier – Brigadier-General J. D. Heriot-Maitland; and their colonel was invested with the order of St Stanislaus, third class – thus did the Czar remember his allies.

The official war diary tells of football matches behind the lines, and such luxuries as a day when the whole battalion enjoyed a proper bath at Gaudiempe.[3] Other medals were presented at suitably con-vened parades, and they were inspected by their corps commander (Lord Cavan).

By October they were back in the Albert sector of the Somme front, returning from the river Couche where they had spent Septem-ber. Taken out of the line, they trained for a major assault on Gommecourt, in which in the event they did not participate, and then went back into the line at Les Boeufs near Albert.

Here five days were spent making minor 'trench straightening' attacks resulting in three officers[4] and nineteen men being killed and one officer and forty-seven men being wounded.

Most of November was spent out of the line; then on 9th December they were to experience another of the Tommies' set hates – namely taking over French trenches. Despite the fact that the war was on their own soil, the French adopted a much more lackadaisical attitude to day to day warfare than we did.[5] (The Germans considered us particularly ferocious in comparison; and the 'live and let live' attitude (so frowned upon by the British High Command) was much more prevalent among the French. As a consequence, when in the line the average *poilu* devoted his time to staying alive until he was relieved, and little or no work was done in repairing or maintenance of the trenches. By our standards, many were particularly disgusting, and as a result Tommy found he had even more work to do than usual in trying to improve the conditions he inherited.

Out of the line again, and then early on Christmas morning they relieved the 4th King's Regiment in the front line at Rancourt. The weather was ghastly and the trenches so muddy that all movement by day was impossible. A not at all happy Christmas[6] made memorable that evening by a Russian prisoner who had escaped, making his way successfully through the German front line, across no-man's land and then safely into 'B' Company's front line trench.

Boxing Day saw, in terms of exchange of fire, one of the hottest days of the war that the battalion ever experienced in a quiet part of the line, with aircraft from both sides very active. So much for the spirit of the unofficial Christmas truce of two years before.

On leaving the line on the 29th, they suffered a gas attack.

There was more training in the very heavy snow already referred to, and then they were back into the line at Clery-sur-Somme on the last day of the month.

On 5th February, Lieutenant J. G. Brown[7] (Suffolk Yeomanry) and three other ranks were killed repulsing a particularly savage German trench raid.

Stormont Gibbs: At Clery-sur-Somme there is a very minute railway station. It had at this time a building with no roof, a grass-grown rusty siding (*voie de garage*, I think is the expression) containing one derailed disintegrating goods truck. The railway runs along the river towards Péronne which was some miles behind the German line –

and reminiscent of *Quentin Durward*. When the wind was east one was supposed to hear the chimes of a Péronne clock.

A valley runs from the neighbourhood of Combles southward to the Somme. Up this valley were earth tracks well worn into ruts by the transport at some previous stage. East of the valley on the ridge ran the front line, with the German trench on the side unable to overlook our territory. The ridge ends abruptly with a steep bank down to a road and the railway beyond which is the marshy margin of the Somme which is wide at this point – (perhaps $\frac{1}{4}$ mile including swamp and high rushes?). Across the Somme was the French Army: we were the extreme right battalion of the BEF. In the said bank was the Battalion HQ – a good deep RE-constructed dug-out, dry but a bit lousy. It was a quiet piece of the line when we took over. There was a full moon and a clear starry sky. As wars have a job to spoil rivers it seemed an exceedingly beautiful place. I spent much of the first night outside soaking in the glory of the moonlight on the water. It was very peaceful, with an occasional distant explosion just to heighten the romance by recalling that in contrast to the beauty of nature there were two lines of men stretching hundreds of miles in each direction waiting to be told to kill each other. And here flowed the Somme sublimely indifferent to it all.

Next day I remember some signalling officers from Division coming up with a new-fangled arrangement for sending messages back to Brigade. I think it was some sort of primitive wireless set. But anyhow it didn't work and the 'Old Man' certainly didn't offer the men a drink.

Some further mention should now be made of the Colonel, for as Adjutant he now begins to figure very largely in 'my war'. I suppose he was only in his early fifties but he seemed as old as the hills. Every officer and man was completely terrified of him. He was completely tireless and completely fearless. He went through the war with a double rupture and no one ever knew. He neither drank nor smoked, didn't allow anyone else to in his HQ, was never known to offer anyone a drink or anything else, nor could any other members of HQ mess do so. He would not feed with, or tolerate in his HQ, anyone but the three necessities, the Adjutant, the MO and (when not in the line) the Second-in-Command. Bombing officers, Lewis gun

67

officers, signal officers, etc., if he had to have such reptiles in his battalion, could form a 'B' mess and make themselves scarce. What was the good of them? And certainly he saw to it that in our battalion at least they were completely useless.

Colonel Copeman had shared a study at Sandhurst with Allenby and started the war as only a major. He had served many years in India (after going through the Boer War) and came home a mere captain. A disappointed man makes a rare martinet. And just as an insignificant office clerk will return from the City and visit the snubs and rebukes of his employer upon his helpless family, so did the 'Old Man' bully his regiment, as he considered that now by rights he should have been an Allenby. It is hard to realise that 'it is not in our stars but in ourselves that we are underlings'. While Allenby was helping to win the war, Copeman was cursing his quartermaster for losing the fork or the blanket that he had used in the Boer War. To me he was alternately kind and considerate and a demon, according to mood. The MO, my best friend and companion, since leaving Rash and 'B' Company, lived in holy terror of him. Of these various people more later.

Editor : Shortly after the war Stormont Gibbs paid an impromptu social call on Colonel Copeman at his Suffolk home. He was undoubtedly looking very much the scruffy undergraduate in rather a dilapidated motor car. The butler took one look and relegated him to the tradesman's entrance. However, when the mistake had been rectified, he was not only well received but was both astonished and gratified to find that his petrol tank had been filled prior to his departure.

Stormont Gibbs : The day after our establishment in the line at Clery an unpleasant thing happened. There was a man in the battalion who had run away on numerous occasions. His intelligence was low and he could not stand war at all. After, I think, the sixth occasion when he had collected some twenty years or more 'penal servitude' from various courts martial, I made him my servant so that he shouldn't have to go in the line. Officers' servants were always left behind at transport lines – I can't think why.

The unfortunate man then proceeded to run away from transport lines. He was court-martialled and condemned to be shot. We were ordered to supply a firing party. I sent a chit to OC Companies to supply a few men each – wondering what would happen. As I expected, everyone refused to do it and I wasn't going to press the company commanders on the subject. I rang up Brigade and had a rather heated conversation about it and finally the poor chap was shot by someone else – perhaps by a well-fed APM, such as C. E. Montague describes. I had to write to the man's mother.[8]

On the following day the divisional commander woke up with a bright notion that some little feat of daring would enhance the prestige of his division – and perhaps his own. The line was far too quiet for our fiery major-general. What about a little raid and a prisoner or two for the corps' cage? So he enquired after breakfast of his DAAG (no, it is a better one than that but I forget the expression) who was in the front line by the river. '4th Suffolk, sir.'

Good enough – we were to raid that night, bring in prisoners and the maps, etc., which were liable to be in the German company HQ at a point somewhere in the middle of their front line. My first really foul job as Adjutant was to select the company to make this raid, for it was tantamount to selecting the officer who would lead it. Actually of course it was the CO's orders but the Adjutant keeps the roster and advises and is in fact sort of 'Secretary of State' as far as responsibility goes in some things. 'B' Company had to do it – my own old company – and the officer was 'Bunny' Bennett, one of the batch of officers who came to us from the Queen's Regiment because we had used up all our reserve officers from our home battalions at Halton.

I had to spend a morning with Bennett with maps and plans drawn in the sand working out just what he was supposed to do. It was terrible because he was simply dithering with fright and neither of us thought he had much chance of getting through. An officer stood a very poor chance always.

We were to be given artillery preparation and a creeping barrage which would lift after so many minutes when it was calculated the party would be ready to jump into the German front line.

When night came my small part in it was over as I sat in the perfect stillness outside the Battalion HQ in the slightly cloudy moonlight thinking of Bennett a hundred yards ahead getting ready. I shall always remember waiting for the barrage to start. Not a sound all along the line. Then on the stroke of zero hour one solitary gun. Then in a couple of seconds hell's own pandemonium let loose. At first just on our divisional sector, then taken up all along the line, spreading to the French beyond the river and for all I know to the English Channel in the other direction. Bennett was off and there followed nearly half an hour of suspense, I should say, with everyone who had cover getting into it and the earth trembling with explosions.

About dusk there had been a slight modification of plans. A large half-caste looking fellow shoved his head in our HQ. He was the brigade trench mortar officer and specialised in shooting large bombs from positions near our front line into the enemy front line. He had been sent up to help the raid, he said, and had got an emplacement for his mortar or mortars at a certain point which he indicated. 'Can you be sure of reaching this point from there?' I said, indicating the spot where we were to enter the enemy trench. 'Yes, easily.' I wondered – I mistrusted the infernal machines. However, I sent the brigade officer up to 'B' Company HQ with a chit to Bennett and told him to discuss carefully with Bennett exactly what he was going to do. He must be sure to lift when the artillery did; if he couldn't shoot far enough he must stop popping off.

A year later I found this same cove hooking it from a Ypres battlefield when his services were most needed and he nearly got court-martialled. So I have little doubt that on this occasion he merely worked his machine regardless of where he was shooting. Bennett got half-way over and then got one in the back from him. The raid failed. The general cursed. And then my memory fades out with the final scene. I was standing in a communication trench in the dim light. 'Is it — ?' 'Yes, sir, it's Mr Bennett.'[9] The tone of voice left no need to ask if he could speak. I watched the little group disappear down the trench. The guns had ceased and the peace of an hour ago pervaded the calm winter night.

Editor: The CO's official report is worth reading in the light of Stormont Gibbs' words:

Report on Raid Carried Out by the 1/4th Suffolk Regiment

at 9.30 p.m., February 13th, 1917

At Zero the parties who had been formed up in our trench by the gap got out and lay down in front of our wire, in the order in which they were to go over. They followed up the barrage, led by 2/Lieut. L. P. Bennett, and as it lifted the first party got through the German wire, and entered the trench at about 1.7.d.08.65. 2/Lieut. Bennett established his Headquarters at this point, and the first party pushed down the trench to the right (South), under Sergt. T. Lamb. Before they had gone far they discovered a dug-out; they shouted to the occupants to come up and they did so, the first having an overcoat over his head. The party pushed on for at least another 40 yards, meeting little or no opposition, and did not find anything. The prisoners were sent back under an escort of 2 men to 2/Lieut. L. P. Bennett, who sent them under the same escort back to our line. On reaching the enemy wire, a shell or mortar (believed to have been one of our own) fell amongst them and killed them all. (Their remains can be seen in the enemy wire this morning.) Time now about 9.45 p.m. In the meantime the second party had entered the enemy trench directly after the first, and had moved North. Before going far, however, they encountered a strong party of the enemy; these parties bombed each other, and progress became very slow.

The third party got into the trench behind the second party, and, owing to the second party making slow progress, found themselves very crowded.

2/Lieut. A. W. Hare, who was leading this party, pushed forward to discover what had happened to the second party. He succeeded in reaching a small latrine, from which he was able to throw bombs. He considered that altogether the second party must have inflicted considerable casualties on the enemy party, but they were only able to make very slow progress up the trench, one reason for this being that the leading bayonet man of the second party had become a casualty.

The enemy were throwing the majority of their bombs over the heads of the second party into the third party, who were crowded, but the throwing was bad and we sustained few casualties. 2/Lieut. L. P. Bennett, who was controlling the three parties with great coolness, ordered the third party to ease back a little as they were crowded. (Time about 9.48 p.m.)

Shortly after this 2/Lieut. L. P. Bennett was badly wounded in the thigh. This left the parties without a leader, and just then the bugle was blown at the prearranged time. This was unfortunate, as the second party had not had time to make much progress Northwards, owing to the opposition they encountered.

We sustained a few casualties as our men returned to our trench from fragments of shell and mortar.

The strength of the raiding party was 2 Officers and 53 Other Ranks.

Our total casualties amounted to :

1 Officer wounded severely.

1 Other Rank killed.

3 Other Ranks missing (believed killed).

5 Other Ranks wounded.

The Medium T. M. Officer told me yesterday that he had not been able to register before the raid.

(sd) H. C. Copeman, Lieut. Col.,
Commdg. 1/4th Suffolk Regiment.

The battalion then reverted to training behind the line, the most remarkable incident of this time being when a wild boar charged through the column on a route march.

Stormont Gibbs : The next time we came into line at Clery the rivers were frozen across and there was snow. I remember nothing, except that we had to patrol the river in white overalls – not that I had to myself or I should doubtless remember something about it.[10]

And so good-bye to the Somme. To Arras.

NOTES

[1] This was not here or then – he was appointed Adjutant on 1st January the following year at Villers-Sous-Ailly. (Confirmed on 20th March, 1917).

[2] The weather between 31st January and 17th February was indeed very severe.

[3] One of the worst memories of the infantryman was of being permanently filthy and literally lice infested – it was known as being 'lousy'.

[4] Including 2/Lieutenant Geoffrey Adams, already referred to. Stormont Gibbs and Jack Rash were away on a course at this time. The other two were 2/Lieutenant Eric G. Joyce, buried at Guillemont Road Cemetery, and 2/Lieutenant Cecil A. Harris, The Queen's (Royal West Surrey Regiment) attached to the 4th Suffolk, buried at Grove Town Cemetery. Geoffrey Adams has no known grave and is commemorated on the great Thiépval Memorial.

[5] The French Army was to mutiny in 1917.

[6] Christmas dinner was not enjoyed until 6th January.

[7] Lieutenant J. G. Brown (who had voluntarily returned from S. Africa to enlist) is buried at Hem Farm Military Cemetery.

[8] His Honour Judge Anthony Babington, author of *For the Sake of Example*, a history of military executions in the Great War, told me 'That he always wondered how it was possible to persuade fellow soldiers from the condemned man's own battalion to be members of the firing party.' War Office documents of the time gave no instructions for procedures to be followed.

The Judge was granted access to the capital court martial files only on the undertaking that he revealed no names. Following the publication of his book there was speculation in *The Times* that records would be made public, but nothing has happened. The French will make theirs public in 2018, and the German records were destroyed in 1945.

[9] Bunny Bennett died the following day and is buried in Bray Military Cemetery.

Major General R. J. Pinney Commanding Officer of 33rd Division.

CHAPTER FOUR

Arras

Editor : During the comparative quiet of the winter months, the High Command had been taking stock of the situation and the options open to them.

Their calculations showed that by the spring of 1917 they would have an advantage in the ratio 3.9 to 2.5 in men on the Western Front and, with the British war machine now fully mobilised, they had no problems of a logistical nature. They also believed that this advantage was the greatest they were ever likely to achieve because, although the Russian Revolutions still lay in the future, her armies were definitely weakening, and even if America did enter the war (as she did on 6th April), it would be years rather than months before her assistance could be anything but nominal.

The command structures of the Great War were distinctly inferior to those of the 1939–1945 conflict (although it can fairly be argued that it was experience gained from the former that benefited the latter).

On a national level, the communication between the politician on the one hand and the Service chiefs on the other was haphazard, to say the least, and the co-operation between the Allies themselves also left much to be desired. The former was heightened by personal antipathy between Prime Minister Lloyd-George, and the C-in-C on the Western Front, Sir Douglas Haig. This regrettable (because it was to a large extent caused by mutual misunderstanding) animosity was the more serious because each man was in his own way an articulate supporter of two seemingly very respectable but opposing schools of thought on the higher strategy of the war.

There were 'Easterners' who, seeing only deadlock on the Western

Front and an unbelievable slaughter the only consequence of trying to break it, believed that the alternative was to attack Germany's allies, eliminate them from the war, and thus totally surround the main foe. The Gallipoli fiasco of 1915 had rather dampened their enthusiasm for large scale Middle Eastern operations, but the current idea among Easterners was to put our major effort into supporting an Italian offensive against Austria. Lloyd-George was a leading advocate of this school.

The 'Westerners', of whom Haig was not even the most articulate proponent, maintained that there would be no victory over Germany, which is what the public wanted (and let us not forget that, again unlike World War II, there were no definite war aims), until the German Army in the field was defeated, and that whilst the method could certainly be improved,[1] 'side shows' were irrelevant and indeed dangerously weakening to the strategical integrity of France, and therefore the enemy must be sought out where he was (i.e. the Western Front),[2] brought to battle and defeated.

Thus whilst the soldiers (or most of them) thought offensive thoughts in the West, and the politicians (or most of them) sought blindly to restrain them, a general impasse and inertia developed that was to be broken, as is so often the way, by the emergence of one man in one key position.

The French C-in-C Joffre was replaced by General Nivelle.

Nivelle, like so many continentals (and indeed our own Sir Henry Wilson), was as much a politician as soldier. The son of an English mother and therefore fluent in the tongue, he achieved the impossible. He convinced Lloyd-George that he had found the foolproof way to instant breakthrough and victory in the West and indeed all he asked of his British allies was a major diversionary attack in support of his masterpiece.

Lloyd-George, becoming totally captivated with the man, thus broke the impasse by ordering Haig to co-operate. Haig had his doubts – he still favoured (because he was ever 'Neptune's General') an offensive up the Flemish coast in conjunction with the Royal Navy. Thus for the second time he had to fight on ground not of his choosing in deference to the wishes of his allies. This time, for him it was to be Arras; for the French, Champagne.

The Germans meanwhile, fully aware of their disadvantage in numbers, had shrewdly made a strategic withdrawal to brilliantly prepared defences known to them as the Siegfried Line and to the British as the Hindenburg Line. In so doing they systematically laid waste the ground they had abandoned. At a stroke they had shortened their line, put themselves in a position to fight in defences of enormous strength, and created a virtual desert for their enemies to advance across.

The British were to attack the Hindenburg Line on 9th April with one army,[3] so as to draw the German reserves, and the French were to make their knockout assault a fortnight later in Champagne. The 1st Russian Revolution broke out in March, thus altering the entire strategic situation. The plan was not changed.

The battle opened with some limited success. The Canadians, with the loss of 7,000 casualties, even took the notorious Vimy Ridge, which 150,000 Frenchmen had perished trying to take two years before.

However, despite General Allenby's desire for a short preparatory artillery bombardment to achieve maximum surprise, he had been overruled (the General Staff had even promoted his artillery commander in order to replace him with someone of their own orthodox views), and the enemy received ample warning of the impending blow.

Very soon the same old tragic story of the battle becoming bogged down repeated itself. To try and retrieve the situation, General Gough's Fifth Army (which the 4th Suffolk had joined on 9th April) was ordered to join the attack to the south and take up with the Third Army.

Bearing in mind that this attack was launched across the devastated area left by the Germans with virtually no preparation (but therefore with maximum surprise, which vindicates Allenby) it came surprisingly near to success. Urgent necessity even led to an inspired and intelligent role for the tanks, but there were too few of them.

However, albeit temporarily, the Hindenburg Line was breached and taken but, there being no further reserves, most gains had to be abandoned. As a diversionary attack (as planned), it was a success, but a golden opportunity to turn it into something much more was lost through lack of flexibility and forward thinking. The French attack was a total and bloody failure and ended with the mutiny of the French Army.

Let us first read Lieutenant-Colonel C. C. R. Murphy's (himself a Suffolk and regimental historian) account of the 4th Battalion's part in the battle* :

On 11th April, after a tiresome day of waiting, the battalion moved up through Blairville in deep snow to Madeleine redoubt, a system of trenches situated where the Albert–Arras railway crosses the Ficheux–Mercatel road.

On 12th April the battalion moved forward into two hollow roads in front of Neuville-Vitasse, its headquarters sharing with that of the 1st Middlesex Regiment an ample dug-out, large enough to hold at least a hundred men.

On 16th April the battalion began taking over trenches in the Hindenburg line, a slow, laborious relief not completed till the next day. Headquarters and two companies were established in the famous Hindenburg tunnel, which, having a section of nearly seven feet square, ran underground for miles. It was provided with ample recesses, numerous entrances consisting of stairways with thirty or forty steps and iron railings, sleeping-bunks with wire beds, and – at the Sensee valley end – even a water supply. The remaining two companies were in the former German front line, liberally provided with concrete machine-gun posts. Relieved on the 20th, the battalion returned to Neuville-Vitasse, but two days later began moving up into the line again for the second battle of the Scarpe.

Zero hour on 23rd April was fixed for 4.45 a.m., the British troops attacking on a front of about nine miles. The 4th Battalion, with two companies in the front line and two in support, was to attack southwards down its trenches as far as the edge of the Sensee valley, and to link up with a brigade making a frontal attack on that portion of the Hindenburg line still in the hands of the enemy. This being a battle of two dimensions, certain troops were detailed to mop up in the tunnel, but it was an almost impossible

*The History of the Suffolk Regiment 1914–1927. Hutchinson, 1928.

task to drive back the Germans on the surface and under it as well.

At first all went smoothly. The barricades fell, the companies pushed forward gallantly almost to the edge of the Sensee valley, and 650 prisoners, with a *Grenatenwerfer* and five machine-guns, were brought in, seventy prisoners having been rounded up in one tunnel entrance and marched back to the rear[4] by a former Bantam.[5] Success seemed certain. 'A' Company had pressed forward to within two hundred yards of the Sensee valley, 'D' in the support line being about level with them. The enemy, however, now counter-attacked vigorously, and these two companies, being unsupported on their flanks, were compelled to fall back. The tunnel proved to be a source of weakness, for in it, sheltering from the bombardment, was a large force which came up in the rear when the counter-attack began. Part of 'D' Company, having been cut off, withdrew across country in rear of the support trench, where 2nd Lieutenant H. W. Woods was killed. The maze of communication trenches between the front and support lines, which it was impossible to guard or even watch, afforded the enemy excellent cover during his advance. Two companies of the 5th Scottish Rifles came up to support 'C' and 'D' Companies; but it was all in vain, and by 3 p.m. the enemy were back at the barricades of the morning. Twice during the course of the day had battalion headquarters turned out and manned the parapet. Captain J. Gaston, the medical officer, passed through his aid-post men of eight different units.

Another barricade was hastily constructed in rear of the original one. At 6.30 p.m. a fresh attack was actually being launched when it was cancelled. It drew forth vigorous retaliation, but by ten o'clock the firing had once more subsided.

The battalion, having been relieved, moved out at 8.30 a.m. on the 24th. Their astonishment may be judged when, on getting out of the trench in order to pass the barricade built at brigade headquarters in the alarm of the day before, they looked back and saw British troops walking about on the hotly contested ground of the previous day. They then learned that the Germans, evidently hard hit, had withdrawn some distance during the night, and that

Officers, 3/4th Suffolk Regiment – Halton May 1916.

a considerable length of the Hindenburg line had been gained. Their casualties in the struggle for Guémappe on 23rd April amounted to 315, including the following officers: *killed* – 2nd Lieutenant H. W. Woods[6]; *wounded* – Captain J. C. Rash, 2nd Lieutenants A. W. Hare, W. R. Wolton, F. Dallimer, D. Glen, B. C. Rigby, B. S. Evans, and S. C. Williams.[7]

Now to Stormont Gibbs' own narrative :

Stormont Gibbs : In the spring of 1917 the Suffolks went up to Arras from the Somme. In this part of the world was the 'Hindenburg Line', a German defensive system of trenches with a long deep tunnel running some thirty feet below the support trench (i.e. the trench some 50 to 100 yards behind the front line trench). The purpose of this was, of course, to provide complete shelter during the bombardments for all except those actually manning the front line firing posts.

At the part of the line into which we went the German trenches had recently been taken by the British so that their support trench under which the tunnel ran was our front line. The entrances to the tunnel which were shoots at a gradient of say 45 degrees and which occurred perhaps every 40 to 50 yards faced the Germans and an unlucky shell could of course land right into one of these entrances. Steps had been cut in the mud originally, but after the recent rain which had poured down, the steps had more or less disappeared and a slip at the top was liable to mean a slide to the bottom, a process which still further wore away the remains of the steps.

I believe that we occupied the Hindenburg Line from Arras, some miles to the north, down as far as where our battalion went into the line on 21st April. But we were the last battalion on the right (or south) and then a few yards further along was the Bosch – with just our sandbag wall and his, a few yards of no-man's trench between. We connected with no one, in fact, on our right flank – it was 'in the air'. We occupied say 200 yards of front line trench (under which ran the tunnel) and 200 yards of support trench 50 yards behind and parallel. In front of the former was our barbed wire screen and behind the latter was the old German barbed wire. The two trenches were joined at intervals of course by communication trenches.

Further north our front line must have swung out in front of the Hindenburg Line because, as far as I know, only our own battalion actually occupied it and further back in the tunnel was our Brigade HQ. They could certainly not have been in the front line. It must have gone something like this : [see p. 84].

The 4th Suffolk had two companies in the front (with tunnel below) and two in support line. It was the first occasion on which I had been in the line, with a major 'show' in view, as adjutant instead of as a company officer. So that I was in Battalion HQ with the CO and the doctor. Battalion HQ was a small excavation in the side of the tunnel with a blanket separating it from the passage way of the tunnel itself. Alongside was the shoot running up to the trench. Beyond the shoot was the doctor's aid post, a similar excavation occupied by his aid sergeant and orderlies. Beyond that again was the den for the HQ staff of of runners, orderlies and signallers, with telephones connecting us to Brigade HQ a quarter of a mile perhaps further back along the tunnel where, as we had come into the line, we had stopped for a word with the Brigadier and Brigade Major.

On completion of the relief we sat down to a meal around an upturned packing case with candles set about. *Journey's End* provides a description of scenery which fits the case though our HQ mess never ran to whisky or any sort of livening liquor.

As we were finishing the meal the only amusing event of this three-day period in the line happened. There was a sudden woof of air and a simultaneous loud, though somewhat muffled, detonation. All the candles were blown out – apparently as far down the tunnel as Brigade HQ. Someone was sent in both directions to investigate and word came back that there had been a slight accident. One of our men had sat on a live German bomb and it had gone off. Luckily, this was a stick bomb, a kind that makes more noise than destruction and more luckily still the man had placed a full pack on the bomb and then sat on his pack. So that he was more frightened than hurt and was sent off to more pleasant surroundings with only a few bits of tin sticking into his hind quarters.

When reports had come in from companies that all was in order, I doubtless visited companies and got the general geography of the land. Then we probably got some sleep for a few hours. I only recall

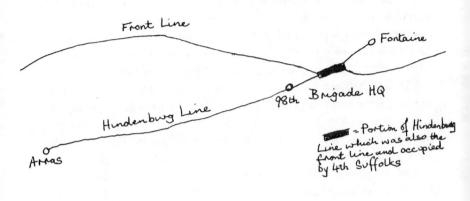

Front Line

Fontaine

98th Brigade HQ

Hindenburg Line

Arras

= Portion of Hindenburg Line which was also the front line and occupied by 4th Suffolks

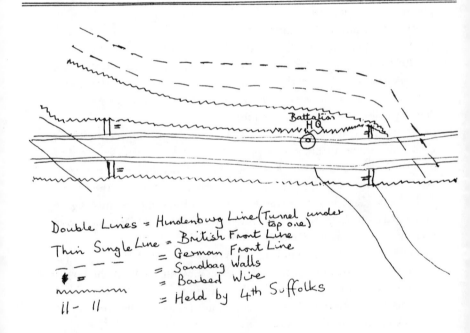

Battalion HQ

Double Lines = Hindenburg Line (Tunnel under top one)
Thin Single Line = British Front Line
= German Front Line
= Sandbag Walls
= Barbed Wire
= Held by 4th Suffolks

Two sketch maps copied by Gibbs' secretary from his originals drawn on lined paper.

the events of the next night : routine in ordinary trench life was fairly sameish.

'Secret and Confidential' letters came up from the Brigade during the day. We were to capture about two miles of line by bombing down the front and support trenches as far as the village of Fontaine-les-Croisilles there connecting with an Australian battalion who were making a frontal attack on the village. This was not incidentally a healthy bit of line where you could stand up and have a good look round. It you could have done so you would not have been able to distinguish the village for it wasn't there any longer. (Today it is a bright little place of new red brick houses with singularly hospitable inhabitants.) So one's plans were made entirely from the map.

Large quantities of bombs were sent up during the day and issued in their boxes to companies. Orders to companies were that the companies should proceed along the trench preceded by a bombing squad who would clear out the enemy.

Here I first came up against the CO as Adjutant. I was a very new adjutant; he was a Boer War veteran. I had, however, learnt at a bombing course how one set about the sort of job that had to be done: he had never used bombs. The orders to companies had to go out under my signature and I felt they were all wrong. Why, I felt, should four companies walk down a trench under the enemy barrage – which would open at once – when only the few men at the head of the columns could actually do any effective work. A bombing squad needed a thrower, carriers and a couple of bayonet men to rush round each traverse after the bomb had landed and burst. No one else could be effective except for replacing casualties and carrying bombs and looking out for a counter raid over the top by the enemy – a most unlikely proceeding. Therefore I said two companies at least should remain in reserve in the shelter of the tunnel – if only to reserve their strength and numbers to meet the almost inevitable counter attack. But I met as on other occasions with, 'Are you commanding this battalion or am I ?' If I had had more experience of the 'Old Man' at that time I should have had a quiet word with Watson, the brigade major, on the phone or hopped back on the quiet to see the Brigadier but, alas, I did not commit this breach of military etiquette. How many lives it would have saved. How bitter I felt after as I looked at the torn bodies of those poor fellows hanging limp in the barbed wire through which they had tried to escape.[8]

Well – by the evening all was prepared for this dawn attack. I went to discuss plans with the subalterns who were to lead the bombing along each trench. There was the inevitable 'nerves' which could take people in so many ways. X was a pleasant man, one of the very few officers the 'Old Man' ever liked, and was to lead along the front line. His 'nerves' took the form of longing to be a dare-devil. It was just dark and he said, 'Let's crawl along outside the trench and chuck a bomb over further down and see what happens.' I said, 'Don't be a fool; it'll only stir up trouble when we don't want it.' However, I was affected with the same feeling and was nearly quite ready to do it until I thought of the fury of the 'Old Man' if either of us got hurt. For we both had somewhat key positions in the events planned for dawn. Strangely it did not occur to me that we might actually get killed even though I had now been in France for eight months. And both X and I were affected by the primitive desire to go crawling on our stomachs and peeping about to see what we could see. Anyhow, I returned to Battalion HQ.

A few hours later news came down that Mr X was lying seriously wounded in no-man's land. So he had done it. Something in my face must have led the 'Old Man' to think I knew something about this. Eventually I told him what I thought had happened. A runner was sent to ask if he could be got in and the answer came back that it was quite impossible. 'I must go and try,' I said. 'You certainly won't,' he said. 'One is enough just before this attack and you certainly can't be spared.' However, after a certain amount of argument, his face softened as just occasionally it could. He was very attached to X. 'All right,' he said. 'Good boy' or words to that effect. I went to the runners' dug-out and asked for two volunteers to help. Two offered and we set off up the tunnel. But there was to be no excitement and I was certainly very glad for I knew we had taken on an almost impossible task. Before we got 100 yards up the tunnel we met a stretcher. He had crawled in. He is still alive minus a leg.[9]

It seems that X had done what he had spoken of with me. He crawled out over the parapet and along level with the German sentry just bomb in hand. But the German heard a noise and threw a bomb at him first.

The attack at dawn started in the approved style. Our barrage opened all along the German line and the Germans mostly took refuge in the tunnel. Then their barrage opened on our trenches and our closely packed companies as they moved slowly forward passing up bombs to the front. I, of course, remained at Battalion HQ with the CO in great safety, for we had for once an impregnable dug-out – apart from a direct hit into an entrance. The attack was only made along the trenches : there was no bombing along the tunnel. But as our men passed each tunnel entrance they had to chuck a bomb down and then go down and kill or capture. At least that was the idea – poor Suffolk peasants.

Our artillery barrage was strong and accurate. It shattered the German positions sufficiently to make things easy and there was little resistance. In what I should guess to be some three hours the 4th Suffolks had taken all their objectives. The chief hero was a very small and young lance-corporal who descended to the tunnel at some point and returned with about seventy prisoners all following him like lambs.

But what a toll of casualties! Our companies had been in the open all the time and back to the aid post poured a continual stream of wounded along the tunnel. The doctor was working incessantly for three or four hours with only a five minute interval to slip into our den and eat a piece of bread and cheese with hands all over blood. I had helped him in intervals of dealing with messages, orders and telephone calls to Brigade. I remember a young corporal coming along with one arm hanging by a piece of flesh and skin. 'Turn your head round, lad,' said Gaston. Then he neatly cut off the arm and threw it under the bench. 'Off you go,' he said as the orderly quietly applied a dressing. And the man, like the rest, would have a mile or two to walk before getting to the Casualty Clearing Station. Then he would have found ambulances full of stretcher cases. This instance only comes to mind among the continual procession of wounded men because I marvelled at the doctor's cheery callousness in this shambles. I was only just learning myself how to protect my own nerves in a similar fashion.

The wounded were nearly all walking cases of course. A stretcher case does not stand much chance in a 'show' like this. They have to wait and usually die. For there are only a few stretcher bearers to each company and if they go off with a wounded man for an hour or two it doesn't do. Also a stretcher coming down impedes ammunition going up.

When it was reported that our objectives had been reached there was a lull, an ominous lull. We calculated that not more than half the battalion could be left – to hold two miles of trench. We asked for reinforcements. None were forthcoming. Presumably the enemy would counter-attack and try to win back what he had lost.

I do not remember what time of day it started. But when the enemy was assured that the trenches in question were definitely taken by us and that none of his own men were holding out anywhere he opened his barrage on our poor remnants and put in a fresh lot of troops to drive them back.

Our men in the support trench held their ground and those in the front trench (with tunnel below) were gradually driven back. Again the wounded started pouring in. And soon came the news that we had no one left in the front trench – all were wounded or madly trying to escape with the wounded. Then came the report that our bombs which we kept hurling up to the front were duds. They were not exploding for they had not been detonated. A Mills bomb has a small detonator which is inserted at the ammunition dump under Brigade supervision before being sent up to the infantry. We had received a large number of bombs which had not received their detonators and so were useless – enough to cause a débâcle, especially when the men were exposed to heavy artillery bombardment and had been reduced by casualties to a handful.

When the enemy had driven us back for a considerable distance along our front line he was of course able to work down the communication trenches and get in behind our men who were holding their own in the support trench. When these were attacked in front and behind they tried to save themselves by bolting across the open. But they ran into barbed wire and were mopped up to a man by machine-guns.

Thus by late afternoon there was literally no one left between the

Battalion HQ and the enemy. Evidently the enemy were not aware of this for they worked their way back quite slowly along the trenches they had re-won.

It is at this point that I had time to take stock of my own situation and my sensations remain very vivid. At Battalion HQ there were the CO, myself, the doctor, still working away with the more seriously wounded who were crowding up every niche and cranny in the tunnel, a couple of orderlies, a couple of signallers trying to repair the wire back to Brigade and a mess cook. We had no bombs and no ammunition worth speaking of, no bayonets, a few damaged rifles. But the CO and I each had a dozen or so rounds of revolver ammunition. Between Brigade HQ and the enemy there was just a little party – and the telephone was down. If the Germans had known they could have walked along and taken a brigadier and then gone on and got behind our other troops on the left and cut them off.

I could see myself no reason why the enemy should not do this. Surely they would come on until they met with effective resistance. And therefore for the first time I got real panic. Surely for me this was the end. There could be no way out.

The Brigade must be told the exact situation. I was in the signallers' den trying again at the telephone with no effect. A runner must be sent. It would not take long and perhaps I could thus avoid what seemed certain death. I stood in the tunnel hesitating. Watson, the brigade major, was said to be the ugliest man in the Army – he was certainly one of the best. I valued his opinion. What would he say? He would know I had run back to escape and he would be quite kind. But I could not do it. 'Public school' came uppermost! It just wouldn't be done.

I stood in that tunnel and prayed that God would get me out of the mess somehow and that He would achieve for me the impossible as I learnt then and on subsequent occasions that He can. Looking back, of course, it all seems quite easy. At the time it did just seem to me impossible that I could get out alive.

I rejoined the CO after sending back a full report to Brigade. He evidently felt the end of the war for us was approaching. He never showed fear but on an occasion of this sort he always changed and behaved in a human and cheerful manner instead of his usual rather fierce and surly way of carrying on. 'Well,' he said, 'they won't be here just yet but we had better get ready for them. We have got two men each; one of us must hold the front trench and the other the support.' We got our four men and went up out of the tunnel. Away down towards Fontaine, bombs were exploding intermittently as the enemy worked his way along against no resistance. We decided that I should stay in the transport line with the mess cook and a runner. The CO would go down with the other two men and take the support line. I went back to have one more try on the phone. This time they had got it through; a sweating signaller was there who said he found the break nearly back as far as Brigade. So I got through to Watson who had just got my report. His cheerful matter-of-fact voice was good to hear. 'So you've got to save the 33rd Division from disaster, have you? Well, you'll have a job but good luck!' And then he added, 'We are filling both trenches and the tunnel with barbed wire just in front of Brigade so that will probably stop them till we can get more troops up.' That was quite useful to know, though it did not affect us because we should be dead before the enemy reached that wire.

Then I looked at Gaston. 'Here's a gun for you, Doc. You stay down here and bang it off along the tunnel when you hear them coming. It may stop them a bit.' 'Right you are, lad. I will if I get time.' And then he shouted out some good Irish encouragement as I scrambled up into the trench again. I disposed of my army as follows. I made a niche for myself almost on top of a traverse where I could, by raising my hand, see and shoot down into the bay beyond. At the entrance to that bay I then made a rough sandbag barricade sufficient to make a man pause to climb – so as to give me a stationary target. Behind me I also put some sandbags as some protection against bombs thrown beyond me. Anything coming quite close might conceivably be chucked back as they were using egg bombs with fairly delayed fuses. The two men I put in a traverse behind me, to come into action if I was knocked out. For my revolver in that situation would be worth more than a rifle and at that range I was safe not to miss.

Preparations made, we waited. There was not much danger from shell-fire for the enemy gunners could not tell just how far their men had got and we were so close to the enemy that all the shelling was behind us. On the other hand since Brigade had got our report and knew the situation they had been able to put one gun to fire heavily on the advancing enemy. This was very fortunate because the explosion of shells concealed from the enemy the fact that we were meeting with no actual resistance by bombs. They probably expected to meet someone round each corner they went, though really no one was there. So I sat as the evening drew on. Slowly but surely the enemy came on. The bombs could be seen rising and heard falling, getting always nearer until at last they reached the spot where must have been the remnants of their sandbag wall and perhaps they guessed they had re-taken all the ground they had lost. Would they come on?

I sat with revolver aimed at the next corner round which they would have to come. How long I don't know. Certainly till after dark. And there lamely the story ends in a complete memory fade-out.

We six were, of course, relieved during the night by another battalion – six hundred or so relieving six – and hazily I remember calling in at Brigade HQ on the way down.

When a few days later I heard I had been given an MC, it struck me that there was considerable irony in these things. For I had done nothing much except to feel extremely frightened while others who had deserved the VC perhaps were dead or unnoticed. However, I could feel that on the Somme I had deserved it as much as many of the people who got it, so I did not let it trouble me.

As to the 'value' of an MC at this stage of the war – in our battalion there had only been about one so it was a bit of a 'thing'. Our CO would never recommend for an award unless he felt he had to. In the Army as a whole it was still fairly rare. An officer would regard it as of more merit than an international cap. How strange that seems in peace-time! In the war you could have an international footballer in your regiment without knowing he was there – in France that is – and often a games celebrity was not a star in military things – vide once more *Journey's End*.

As I write of these far-away events I wonder if they all happened in another existence. I can't really believe they happened to me.

Sundry things came back to me as I write which I had forgotten till this moment. I see Jack Rash limping back down the trench with

(2)

quite warm again today

We have had a most excellent home made for us and it is really quite good for the British (General!!!!) H.Qs must make themselves comfortable even in the line. as well as Harwich

You will be pleased to hear that Gibbs the Adjutant and two other officers in the Battalion have got M.C.s for the last show which is very bon!

Tell Harcourt that I will write to him when I get out of the line and I may be able to see him but of course I dont know

Later By the way before I forget will you send me out my other

Part of a letter home to his parents from Lieutenant Horace Brown, MC.

a wound never to return to France. It took the rest of the war to get his leg right. All our officers were new, drafted in from all sources, many not Suffolks at all. Now in a few days we should have to have another lot. In a few days we should be in the line again with new officers and for the most part new men all hastily trained and more hastily absorbed.

Adams and Parry-Crooke had not yet come out to France and I felt I might have been there a hundred years instead of eight months.[10]

The only element of permanency in the battalion seemed to be the CO, the Doc (who then was quite new), Richards, the transport officer, and old Hudson, the quartermaster. The last two were more or less non-combatants and so liable to be safe, though Richards had times of great danger bringing up rations when we were in the line.

It was always good to get back to 'B' Echelon after a time in the line – especially after a 'show' in the line. There was my welcoming orderly room staff, Sergeant Rowe, Corporal Herring and the two clerks – always more welcoming because they themselves remained behind in safety with their typewriters. As I sank worn out in my office chair, or whatever substituted for one, after an all night march from the trenches Sergeant Rowe used to radiate sympathy and cups of tea without ever speaking a word.

The trying thing for an adjutant was that after his time in the line he could not rest like the others, for he had to start at once organising the drafts to replace casualties, writing reports, seeing people, talking on the telephone, dictating to typewriters, arranging billets, huts, tents, supplies, perhaps even attending courts martial. So he might well have several nights in the line with nearly no sleep and then come back to full days of office work, training and parades and more interrupted nights with phone calls from Brigade about the next move.

It was only every ten weeks or so that the whole division might go into 'rest' right behind the line even in billets. Then one got one night's sleep and during the day training, parades and inspections and all the red tape and what-nots of normal military life. These parades as adjutant were not my strong point because I rode badly and had always a curious succession of fiery and uncontrollable steeds. I liked drilling – but battalions with horses involved – no!

But – to revert – the other thing I remember about 23rd April is the fact that tanks were first used by our division. At least two were supposed to help us take that two miles of trench. But they only reached the starting point, then stuck and remained as derelict landmarks for weeks.

I also remember that this Hindenburg Line was an unusually smelly one. Many had been killed in it and lay just beneath the surface of the trench floor or in the walls. The tramp of feet exposed them or bits of them and the weather was warm.

NOTES

[1] Haig, himself, described by one of the, if not the, most knowledgeable living World War I historians as 'The Educated Soldier', was, contrary to popular myth, a most progressive man towards new ideas and tactics and weaponry. With Kitchener (who instantly saw the potential) he must take more credit for the development of the tank than any other senior officer. The fact that he failed to listen to advice on their first tactical use does not mean that he did not learn. Indeed, hard though the lessons were, throughout the war Haig constantly learnt from mistakes – and kept his nerve in hours of crisis. It is really extraordinary that this administratively capable cavalry officer, whose training and thinking were orientated to policing a Colonial Empire should at the war's end receive the accolade from Ludendorff, considered by most the greatest soldier of the war, 'That he – and he alone – stood master of the field'.

[2] There were in fact eight theatres of war or 'fronts' in the Great War. But five out of eight British soldiers were fighting for the majority of the time on the Western Front.

[3] Third Army – General Allenby, later of Palestine fame.

[4] When asked how he managed to collect so many prisoners he replied that 'he had surrounded them'.

[5] Bantams were tiny (in terms of height) soldiers who had originally been rejected by the Army. Later they were allowed to form their own Bantam battalions. Hilarious, but at the time probably not so funny, stories were told of these little warriors relieving Guards' battalions in the line. So great was the height differential that the short newcomers could not even see over the parapet from the fire step. By 1917 these men had been absorbed into normal battalions.

[6] Harold Woods is buried in Cojeul British Cemetery, St Martin-sur-Cojeul.

[7] The battalion was so short of officers that apart from the CO, adjutant, signals officer and MO, only fifteen front line officers were available of whom nine became casualties.

[8] Perhaps the words of Wilfred Wilson Gibson sum up his feelings in his poem, 'We who are left'.

[9] It has been impossible to identify this officer.

[10] Quite wrong. G. Adams was already dead. C. P. Parry-Crooke was not in this battle and was presumably either away on leave or on a course.

CHAPTER FIVE

Summer 1917

Editor : The period between the end of April 1917 and September of that year, when the battalion was committed to the full horror of the Third Battle of Ypres, was another relatively quiet time in the line with longish periods behind it training, absorbing new drafts and as far as possible resting. The battalion received, quite rightly, the personal congratulations of both its brigade and divisional commander for its conduct on St George's Day. General Pinney awarded many medals including the Military Cross to Stormont Gibbs[1] and the MO, Captain Gaston.

Cricket matches were played and the battalion even took part in a gymkhana organised by the brigade. Leave was given – concerts by the divisional band were attended. But there were also times in the line. On 20th May the 33rd Division made a full scale attack on a section of the Hindenburg Line. This time the 4th Suffolk were lucky – in reserve. The attack succeeded without their even being required to leave their trenches. However, a few days before they left the Arras sector on 27th June they endured a terrible bombardment in which 2nd Lieutenant W. Haynes was among those killed.[2]

The battalion spent the month of July back on the Somme before moving up to the Ypres sector on 31st July, where action leading to what is now known as the Third Battle of Ypres had already started with the attack on Messines Ridge on 7th June.

In his memoirs, Stormont Gibbs reminisces mainly about his horse.

After April 1917

Stormont Gibbs : As the war proceeds I am able to be far less chronological and all sorts of memories are mixed up. By reference to scrappy diaries and with much labour they could perhaps be sorted out. But these notes are being written entirely from memory. There are a few special exceptions that can be fixed on to exact dates such as our share in the Third Battle of Ypres in September 1917 and the March Retreat in 1918. These will be dealt with as special stories. I now propose to deal with sundry events of little interest between the spring of 1917 and that of 1918.

After Arras I believe Parry-Crooke and Geoffrey Adams came out from England.[3] Almost before I had seen them, Rash and I went off together on a 'refresher course' for several weeks. We were sent mainly for a rest. I can remember nothing whatever about this period except that it was a little boring. The course was as useless as most, I believe, and we really wanted to get back to the battalion.

It has been queer seeing P-C and Adams arrive and having them report to me as Adjutant. Adams had been senior prefect at Radley and captain of cricket when I was very small fry, and at Halton I was many months their junior and very junior at that. Now I was a veteran of the standing of two or three first-class battles and the feat of surviving more than one was quite rare in those times for an infantry officer. People have little conception of the enormous percentage of casualties among infantry officers on the Somme.

Geoffrey Adams was a very remarkable person who would have had a great career as a barrister – a wholly admirable person whom one may read of in memories by the headmaster of Radley. While Rash and I were away the battalion went into the line again on the Somme for a week at Les Breufs, a quiet sector then for the Somme battle was over. But Adams was sent with a few men in broad day-light to take a machine-gun. None of them survived. The job was impossible and should never have been allowed. One can blame, one can regret, but there it is – and so when we returned there was no Geoffrey Adams. There was a sadness and bitterness felt over this that no words can describe.

An adjutant, being one of the 'mounted' officers of a battalion, has a horse and groom. He only merits these when the battalion is out at 'rest'. In our battalion the CO never rode on a long march – so no one else could. He always walked when his men had to walk and the horses of officers came along with the transport. I only had to use a horse in fact on battalion parades when we were right back in billets and if I had to go somewhere alone or with the CO on duty or merely for a ride.

I had never learnt to ride properly. As a child of seven I had a pony that used to throw me off and this probably started a dislike for riding. I preferred driving it in the pony cart. So partly as a result of this I had a variety of unpleasant experiences with 'Kitty', though she must take some of the blame for she could be a devil. When Kenneth Turner was Adjutant, he had Kitty, and she was then renowned for various feats hardly to her credit. She had on one march plunged into a party of cycle orderlies and put her feet through the wheels of six of the battalion bicycles. It was a question of whether I should have Kitty, but she was the Adjutant's horse and that was that. I didn't much care for her reputation though I imagined the stories of her exploits to be mostly exaggerated. I certainly did not think I should have several narrow escapes from death apart from sundry other exciting experiences as a result of Kitty and my own bad riding.

Adventure No 1 : Riding along a narrow lane on a very dark night – hedge on one side, ditch on the other, beyond ditch a Nissen hut showing dim light. Motor lorry heard approaching, no lights, of course. I could not get off the road or give warning of my presence. I drew Kitty in as close to the ditch as possible. Lorry going by touched her nose with a flapping piece of canvas : she plunged up on hind legs. I clung on and doubtless pulled her higher and she went clean over backwards into the ditch with all legs sticking straight up in the air. I got miraculously thrown clear. Kitty then scrambled up and walked straight in at the low door of the hut where a number of men were sitting round a coke stove. There she stood quite still with her legs wide apart, head down, nostrils distended puffing like St George's charger gazing at a dragon. The effect on the men can be left to the imagination – also my undignified extraction of Kitty from the hut.

Adventure No 2 : Exploring with the CO alone – both mounted – no grooms – no one within miles. Country a mass of tangled barbed wire and telegraph wire much of it overgrown with nettles. Kitty catches her foot in some barbed wire and starts plunging about. The 'Old Man' starts bellowing at me for being a rotten rider. I dismount to disentangle Kitty. Kitty puts over the worst of all her tricks. She walks backwards with her head down pulling and kicking at intervals thereby pricking herself on the wire and getting further entangled. Then she starts circling in the same position, I, holding the reins being thte pivot. I soon become entangled in wire, Kitty goes round and round plunging more and more. This goes on for some minutes to the accompaniment of instructions from the 'Old Man' to do this, that and the other. He had taken his horse clear of the wire area and is secretly enjoying my extreme discomfiture. For now as Kitty goes round, my legs are wound with wire and bound together tightly until I fall down flat and let go of the reins. But the wire which binds my legs together is also round Kitty's back legs. She turns and makes off dragging me feet foremost along the ground kicking at me at intervals. Well – the wire broke! I was a good deal cut about and hurt – so much so that the story which is vivid in my mind fades right out at that point.

Adventure No 3 was the worst though shortly told. Riding along a leafy lane in the quiet country occupied by our heavy artillery. A completely camouflaged gun let off by a humorous gunner just as Kitty and I are within a few feet of it. Kitty off like a streak. Bit between her teeth and going as if all the devils were after her. Straight across a field, Kitty quite blind to all ahead, I able to see wire and shell holes and then suddenly a deep pit straight ahead. She made straight for this pit. I remember taking one rein in both hands and pulling her head round sideways and still she went on. Memory fades as I shut my eyes within a few feet of the pit.

I had many pleasant rides on Kitty but these ordinary things do not remain in the memory. One humiliating experience is quite vivid still – a battalion parade right back at rest billets. For certain movements the adjutant has to give a distant point; he has to gallop say a hundred yards and then stay at a point to mark the direction of the movement. Well, the thing about Kitty was that if I wanted her to gallop she just wouldn't : she just put back her ears and walked slowly making a savage sort of face or tried to bite your leg when she got a dig in the ribs.

The CO gave the order, I remember, and I started off at a jerky sort of walk in the proper direction, digging at Kitty and probably flapping the reins about and making clicky noises intermingled with curses. The battalion watched, the CO watched, getting that explosive expression on his face. But instead of the usual explosion he merely remarked loudly and to the multitude in general, 'Look at the Adjutant riding a horse.' Then after a few seconds he went off with a bang – 'Gallop, man.' Kitty did. Perhaps she thought it was another gun behind her. I lost both stirrups and my tin hat went off the back of my head and hung by the strap round my neck. When I got to laughing distance, I laughed and laughed until Kitty got fed up and stopped. Then I rode sheepishly back on parade and everyone spent a difficult few minutes trying not to catch anyone else's eye while the 'Old Man' glared round waiting for anyone to flicker an eyelid.

Perhaps this is the place for the story of Kitty at High Wood in 1918. We were back near the Somme but the front line was many miles east of the 1916 line and the old battlefields were quiet and deserted – no soldiers, no peasants, no beasts or birds, no living trees. An occasional ammunition dump but that about all as far as one could see across what once would have been described as rolling downs. Utter solitude.

I rode on Kitty one day to visit High Wood – perhaps a five-mile ride from our camp. I wanted to find if Norton and the others had ever been found and buried. I tied Kitty to a stump and explored the battleground which was a mass of little wooden crosses. Many were now rotting and illegible and anyhow I could find none that I was looking for.

I gave it up when the light began to fail and started off home on Kitty. She didn't seem quite herself and suddenly I began to be aware of the intense quiet and loneliness of this land of the dead. How Kitty and I reacted on each other and whose fault it was I don't know but suddenly she began to snort and then off she went like a streak and galloped uncontrollably for miles – 'because he knows some frightful fiend doth close behind him tread'.

La Panne and Maison Rouge
Stormont Gibbs: It was, I expect, soon after the battle of Arras that we went north to Flanders.[4] But before we went we should have

continued going in and out of the line on the Arras front for some weeks perhaps. One such occasion comes to mind. We were in support just behind the position we had occupied in the Hindenburg Line for the battle – just behind the barbed wire through which our people had tried to escape across country. Battalion HQ was a shallow dug-out but dark and offensive and the first summer weather had come. We had nothing to do and the 'Old Man' was in an evil frame of mind. So I sat in the sun on the top of the dug-out though there was a fair amount of desultory shelling going on. I remember being torn between the lovely weather and the knowledge that it was wrong to take unnecessary risks. Then there was a bang nearby and I got a smack in the back that sent me below quickly. It was a piece of shell the size of a tooth that had gone through my clothes and just drawn blood. 'Why can't you stay down here?' growled the 'Old Man'. I had learnt what it felt like to be frightened of the animate enemy, their bombs and their bayonets, but I still had a somewhat scornful attitude towards shells that come from a distance. There is no personal malice about a shell whereas in any sort of hand fighting there are the savage emotions which motivate the shot or thrust. The great horror of war is this prostitution of civilised man. He has to fight for his country and to do so he has in actual practice to be brutalised for his country; he has to learn to hate with the primitive blood lust of the savage if he is to push a bayonet into another human being (who probably no more wants to fight than he does). Need he hate? In the case of the average man he must as the counter-balance to fear. It may be, of course, it probably is, only temporary hate which his thoughtful country helps to work up by a dose of rum. The fact remains, as I see it, that your country for its own interests (a country only fights in its own interests) reverses the commandment and says, 'Thou shalt murder' – 'and learn to do it scientifically, my boy'. Well, why shouldn't any other commandment be reversed in the supposedly national interest? They mostly are from time to time!

Anyhow, shells aren't human and I found them less terrifying for a long time. It took Polygon Wood to break my nerve in the following September and then I felt that anything would be better than that shattering bombardment.

A few days later the CO got sacked by the Brigadier, I imagine for the débâcle in the Hindenburg Line – for it was a bad piece of work keeping no reserves in hand. What a day that was. He opened the letter and crumpled it up and sat and trembled. The Doc and I were heartily thankful, but it was one time we were really sorry for him. He got on his horse and rode off and the Doc was convinced that he was going to shoot himself. We had an anxious hour or two. Then he returned with triumph. He had ridden to Division, seen the Divisional General (with whom he had been at Sandhurst) and got him to go back on the Brigadier. There was no love lost between General Maitland and the 'Old Man' after that.

It was a hot May. In a rest behind Arras – was it at Hendecourt – the name seems to fit? I had an old bath behind the orderly room and used to lie in it up to my neck in cold water. It was here I first got to know Richards, the transport officer. He introduced me to Troward's books and I remember how odd it seemed to find an officer who read a book, especially one called *Bible Mystery*. It was here probably that Hugh Sykes came out.[5]

The Albert Road

Stormont Gibbs: I do not know when it was that we found ourselves on the Albert–Amiens Road with Battalion HQ in a dug-out in the bank at the roadside, on a rise which overlooked the country nearly to Albert itself which was just in German hands. But as I see it now the wheat was ripening so it must have been August 1917 and we must have gone there after La Panne, etc., on the coast and before going to Ypres.[6] The fact that wheat was growing at all five miles behind the line indicates that all was quiet on the Somme front just then.

It was here that we had a near thing in air raids. Battalion HQ consisted of four shallow dug-outs made of circular tin with a few inches of earth on top. One was the mess and CO's quarters: in one slept Doc and I: and the others were occupied by the orderlies and signallers. Enraght was there in some strange capacity – 'Lewis Gun Officer' I expect – and he of course was not tolerated in our mess and had to eat alone. He and I made a dug-out for him and furnished it and decorated it. We had nothing to do and were there for a week. I still have a picture of 'Enny's dug-out'. It was there he made up the famous song 'Beware of Little Frank'[7] (on *Chu Chin Chow* lines).

The Doc and I each had a wire bed with the width of the door between us. We slept head at door end and above my head was a shelf with a heavy telephone instrument – a new contrivance called a Fullerphone. One night we were roused by the sound of bombs and we heard the drone, so easily distinguishable, of an enemy plane coming nearer. Then came the sound of small bombs dropped as feelers each distinctly nearer to us. It was evident they knew our HQ and were making for it. The road made it an easy mark. The last bomb was so close that I decided to turn my head inwards on my bed. As I did so there was a terrific concussion, the whole earth shook and the dug-out was filled with powdered earth and cordite. I was buried in earth as far as the knees and the telephone hurled itself at my head. It was lucky that I had just turned round. A big bomb had landed in the ditch that connected the four dug-outs. Our door was broken in but we could scramble out. The 'Old Man' was quite imprisoned with a large quantity of earth against his door. I got up in the road to find that our rations had arrived at the moment of the raid and there was a dead mule and a dead man and a badly wounded mule. It seemed that I had got to shoot the mule and I didn't know where. Enraght was the prospective vet, so I went to find if he was still alive. He was – but wounded in the right hand. However, I got him to shoot the mule with his left hand before he was tied up and pushed off (with a pleasantly cushy wound he was back again in a few months).

Bombing began to develop at this stage of the war. It was on the July Offensive 1918 that we really suffered from an air raid when French or was it ffrench[8] was killed and all those horses – and Bodger wounded.

La Panne

Stormont Gibbs: And so our time in the Fourth Army came to an end as we were sent up to Flanders. We marched, I think. And for a start they sent us to the seaside at La Panne, an almost undamaged town of some ten(?) miles behind the German Line at Nieuport. (Ostend being well behind the German line.)

Battalion HQ was in a large hotel facing the sea. Only a run down the beach for a bathe before breakfast and a gallop along the sands in the morning. I only remember the luxury of those bathes and rides – never had or has the sea meant so much – for what a contrast. It seemed like a week in heaven might seem after a year in hell. The sea too is a grand mental tonic. The firm-set earth is mutilated by war: everything man can make is smashed by war; but the eternal sea is unchangeable and man cannot affect it with his destruction. And in May the ripples on the hot sands smile. The King of the Belgians lived further along the front: we were supposed to leave cards on him – as though one would be likely to carry cards as part of one's equipment for labelling dead Germans 'bagged'.

I don't think we had more than a week of hotel accommodation. The next thing I remember was being in camp on the dunes at Bray Dunes – and the fleas, a plague of them. Then we went into the line at Maison Rouge. A complicated bit of country, all dykes and canals. Fairly quiet. We had a gramophone at the reserve Company HQ – the tune of the time was 'Let the great big world keep turning'. We ran into Garrard here – an OR heavily decorated and evidently a highly efficient company commander.

I don't remember much of all this. P.C. was now OC 'A' Company, I think. Probably I went on my first leave from here after we had been in and out of the line all about the place for some weeks. (There must be an error in dates – probably we didn't get to La Panne till June.)[9]

Anyhow, I returned from a fortnight's leave to find we had moved down to Ypres and the battalion in support on the Menin Road.

Editor: It was here in La Panne that Stormont Gibbs dealt kindly (by doing nothing) to a very drunk Corporal Whalley who hailed from Southwold. He had met a Belgian fisherman who used to put into that port before the war, whom he knew, and then over-indulged himself in Belgian hospitality as a result of this unexpected reunion.

NOTES

[1] Years later Stormont Gibbs told me that his general had told him that he would arrange for him to receive the medal from the King at Buckingham Palace

on his next leave. Characteristically Stormont protested vehemently that he did not wish this, and so the idea was dropped.

2 William Haynes is buried in Boyelles Communal Cemetery Extension.

3 Again a memory failure – Adams had been dead for eight months and Parry-Crooke had, as we know, come out with Stormont Gibbs himself.

4 The end of July.

5 Yes. Stormont Gibbs subsequently married his sister.

6 This was July 1917 before the battalion went to La Panne. The Albert-Amiens road must have been 1918. The Germans did not capture Albert until March of that year.

7 Major Frank Pretty.

8 Captain Digby M. ffrench killed in September 1918 and buried at Péronne Communal Cemetery Extension.

9 August 1st to be precise.

CHAPTER SIX

Passchendaele

Editor : Along with 'The Somme', the word Passchendaele evokes in an English mind an immediate reaction : it sums up all that is horrific in war. Passchendaele itself is a small village some six miles east of Ypres which has given its emotive name to a series of battles fought in the area in the summer and autumn of 1917 which collectively are known officially as the Third Battle of Ypres.

Before one can even discuss the reasoning and the planning of these actions it is necessary to consider the position of Ypres itself and its 'Salient'.

During the 'Race to the Sea' in late 1914, Ypres, the once prosperous cloth-weaving capital of Flanders, was entered by German cavalry, who were immediately driven out by ours. Although they got perilously close again in 1918, this was the only time the Germans were to enter this town.

Fighting with all the heroism and professional skill that could be expected of any fighting force, the little Regular Army defended the town on a semi-circular line about one and a half miles to its east. It was literally the death of the old Regular Army, but the line held.

Thus the conclusion of the First Battle of Ypres left the British hanging on to an already extensively damaged town and a few square miles of mud surrounding it.

This area is virtually at sea level – indeed Flanders means 'Flooded Land'. The delicate drainage system being destroyed by the holocaust of war, the place quickly became a bog – it was impossible to construct or drain proper trenches. To compound the misery, the Germans overlooked the whole area from a low ridge (itself never more than sixty feet above sea level) which nearly encircled the town[1] to the south. See map on p. 139.)

Militarily it was little less than lunacy to hold on to this quagmire of hell. The logical military solution would have been to withdraw to the high ground around Mount Cassel leaving the Germans to wallow in the unenviable morass below.

However, two facts must be borne in mind. Firstly, the public myth was that we had gone to war to save gallant little Belgium. We held precious little of it, but a withdrawal to the high ground would literally have meant completely abandoning all Belgian soil. Public opinion would never have tolerated that.

Secondly, for most of the duration of the war, we (the Western Allies) considered ourselves to be on the offensive on the Western Front – yielding ground did not figure in offensive thinking in the Great War.

In the spring of 1915 the Germans (in what is known as the Second Battle of Ypres) made another attempt to take the town. It was the first time gas was used in warfare, yet they failed to exploit the gap that this surprise weapon created – the Canadians came up to take the place of the fleeing French Colonial Moroccan troops, and again the line held.

For two years the line remained virtually static – but, unlike other parts of the line, the Ypres salient was never really 'quiet'.

The misery of the living conditions was always made worse by constant shell fire from three directions – forward troops were often shelled from behind (from the Messines area). Places like 'Hell Fire Corner' on the Menin Road had earned their grisly names long before anyone had heard of the word Passchendaele.

It was thus as much to mitigate this constant misery as to prepare for more extensive operations that plans were initiated in mid-1916 to take the Wytschaete–Messines ridge.

This task was entrusted to General Plumer and his Second Army. The absolute epitome (to look at) of Colonel Blimp, this little man was, although the oldest, quite the most capable of all our army commanders on the Western Front.

With meticulous planning and inspired forethought, refusing to be

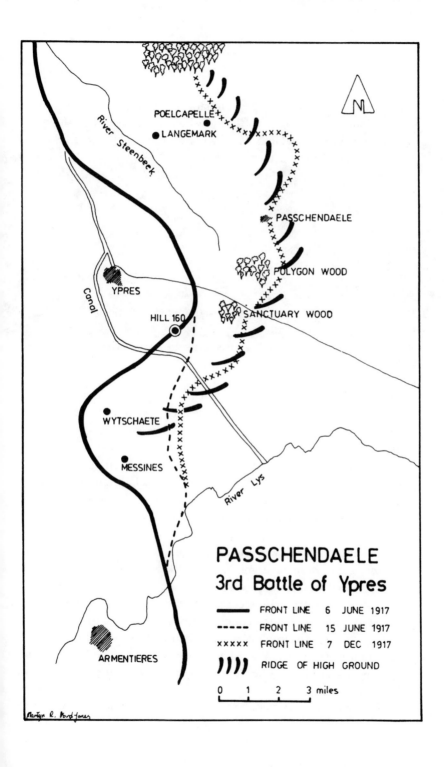

PASSCHENDAELE
3rd Bottle of Ypres

———	FRONT LINE 6 JUNE 1917
- - - -	FRONT LINE 15 JUNE 1917
xxxxx	FRONT LINE 7 DEC 1917
))))	RIDGE OF HIGH GROUND

0   1   2   3 miles

Martyn R. Bord-Jones

Messines Ridge, 11th June 1917. The effects of the bombardment preceding the attack on 7th June.

panicked by the enemy or budged in his plans by others (unlike Allenby at Arras he successfully resisted attempts to remove *his* artillery commander) Plumer had twenty-one great mines tunnelled under the ridge.

The infantry were briefed to the last minute detail and supported by nearly 4,000 guns (which hurled five and a half tons of ammunition per yard at the enemy) and tanks (which in the event were not even required) and placed in their assault positions for H hour long planned for 3.10 a.m. on 7th June.

At that time the air was rent by the flash and roar of nineteen great mines[2] again, as at the Somme, the shock was felt in London – the guns crashed out on a prearranged barrage and before long the advancing infantry had secured all their objectives, killing and taking prisoner vast numbers of enemy at little cost to themselves. It was a very rare example of a classic and perfectly executed military operation in the Great War. The Ypres salient was no longer quite such an awful place to be. (See map on p. 107 – the line on 15th June 1917.)

Meanwhile the Arras offensive – designed originally to be but a

Messines village, lying within the area taken, was almost obliterated.

diversion for the French knockout blow in Champagne – had continued in the dual attempt to exploit successes – in which it failed – and to take the pressure off the French after their mutiny – in which it achieved its object. Now it was drawing to a close.

For the third time General Haig turned his mind and endeavoured to turn other minds to his idea of a great offensive up the Flemish coast in co-operation with the Royal Navy, to outflank the German Army and to clear the Channel Ports, from which U-boats were believed to be operating. This time he was to have his way.

It is terribly easy with hindsight to see the ghastly pitfalls that lay ahead – it would be wiser to recall the words of that shrewd historian F. W. Maitland when he wrote, 'It is difficult to remember that events now far in the past were once in the future.'

There were four factors, which at least at the time were all important – and again let us judge a man on what *he knew at the time* and not on what we know now. Firstly, the coast really did seem the only possibility of opening up a flank and ending the deadlock. Supply problems – enormous in this war – could be to a large extent overcome by the Army's proximity to our superior sea power.

Secondly, the French Army was in a terrible condition, and it was a hard fact of life that the British had to exert tremendous pressure on the Germans somewhere while it nursed itself back to life.

Thirdly, the first Russian Revolution had taken place and likewise the Russian Army was becoming so impotent that already the enemy was able to start moving forces from the Eastern to the Western Front. In the name of that most appositely named of all Great War songs, 'The Yanks are Coming', they were, but they had not come yet. Their commander, General (Black Jack) Pershing, refused point-blank to commit his small regular army piecemeal to combat – but intended (as he did against all protestations) to await the arrival of his volunteers, and then and only then to fight as one great composite army.[3] So in the calculations of mid-1917 they had to be discounted.

Prime Minister Lloyd-George, after Nivelle's disastrous failure, had reverted to his former position of treating with the greatest suspicion offensive operations on the Western Front; but the fourth and at the time most compelling of all factors was suddenly introduced at a top-level conference which included both Haig and himself.

The Admiralty suddenly announced that unless the Channel Ports[4] in German hands were taken extremely quickly and thus the U-boat bases removed we were in immediate danger of losing the war – indeed it was put as bluntly as this : 'We could not go on'.[5]

This new and at the time final consideration made all other arguments seem irrelevant and gave to the undertaking an urgency and a sense of total necessity. With this Lloyd-George concurred and indeed totally identified himself, which made his subsequent (after the war) protestations of non-concurrence dishonourable. Thus we have the strategic backdrop to the tragedy about to be unfolded and can understand its reasoning. Of its tactical implementation we can be justly much more critical.

In my view, whilst there was no alternative to this strategy in mid-1917 for reasons given, I believe that far greater consideration could and should have been given to the choice of ground. We attacked out of the Ypres salient. Between this and the sea stood the tiny Belgian Army with French support. Had we 'passed through' them and literally attacked with the sea as our left flank, I would venture that the story might have had a happier ending. There is no evidence to suggest that the idea was ever considered.

The Battle of Messines had the unfortunate effect of creating expectations that were not to be realised. That battle had been fought with limited objectives in mind – these had been achieved – but it was not or never intended to be a 'break out' battle. The generals of the day were not, unfortunately, able to draw the distinction.

To the total unsuitability for movement (and an attacking army requires to move), owing to the boggy nature of the ground, was added a cruel card dealt by the hand of fate. The summer of 1917 turned out to be the wettest since records had been kept.

The Germans had long anticipated a major offensive here and, overcoming the trench problem, had built massive concrete pill boxes.[6] They were concentrating on holding the ground with machine-gun fire, not men – keeping the latter commodity in reserve for immediate counter-attack.

Thus on 31st July, after a nine-day preliminary bombardment, began the assault which in turn became a series (thirteen in all) of full-pitched battles (known collectively as Third Ypres) that culminated with the final capture of Passchendaele village (and the ridge) in early November.

The conditions were appalling.[7] The casualties were nearly as great as on the Somme. Why, when it became obvious that no break out was going to occur, was it not called off? Because, having got so far, at least let the Army have the luxury of a comfortable winter by taking that accursed ridge and ending the Salient dilemma. Even Plumer concurred in this and it was achieved. One of the greatest Ifs of history is what would have happened had Plumer been in overall tactical command and not Gough – but to explore such Ifs is not the purpose of this book.

Passchendaele – The Suffolks

Editor: The Suffolks spent August in almost unbelievable luxury well behind the line on the coast – although even here they were once shelled (19th August) by heavy 8-inch shells, suffering six wounded. Late that month (23rd–28th) they took over a reserve sector of the line on the British left flank, sustaining not a single casualty and then again back well to the rear until 'their time was come'.

It came on 24th September when the battalion entered the Salient and took over the front line at 'Clapham Junction' (only marginally less notorious than 'Hell Fire Corner') with Battalion HQ in Sanctuary Wood.[8] They then took their full part in the attack on, or battle of, Polygon Wood.

The war diary, as is invariably the way with major battles, tells us little. But there is a surviving report written by the CO. It is worth reading for two reasons : firstly, if only to see the difference between this totally inexplicit load of verbiage so common at the time, and compare it with the professionalism the modern Army would expect (and get) in a report from one of its battalion commanders today: secondly, it does give us an idea of the incredible sense of confusion that prevailed.

Movements of the 1/4th Suffolk Regiment from
24th to 28th September, 1917

'At 7.0 a.m. on the 24th September the Battalion left the bivouac at BELGOED FARM, moving by ZILLEBEKE track to Headquarters of Brigade on the Eastern edge of SANCTUARY WOOD. There the Battalion halted till 1.0 p.m., the C.O. going forward to examine unoccupied trenches "NEW CUT" and "———"[9] crossing the YPRES–MENIN Road roughly at right angles in front of CLAPHAM JUNCTION, finding accommodation for barely 3 Companies. These only moved on at 1.0 p.m., and occupied the trenches. Attempts to improve them were followed by shelling – though after events do not show that it was a case of cause and effect but that shelling was a part of the new offensive of the enemy. The 4th Company remained near Brigade Headquarters. Battalion Headquarters was temporarily in Aid Post at CLAPHAM JUNCTION, as the proper Headquarters were not vacated by the 11th West Yorks Regt. till the evening (C.O. and Adjutant did not leave till 1.0 a.m. 25th). The enemy shelling of the area continued during the night, and increased considerably during the 25th, 2 Company Headquarters being hit (one twice) with 6 fatal casualties.

'Due to circumstances in the front line, the previous orders for the 26th attack were changed, and the Battalion, which in the afternoon had sent forward 1 Company to about J.14 central (LONE LANE) to reinforce 2nd A.&S.Hrs. was ordered to take the ——⁹ originally given to the 1st Middlesex Regt. to attack (from the line to which they had been pressed back in this case) at Zero.

'Later, about 7.0 p.m., the C.O. was called to the Brigade Head-quarters, and received fresh orders to move forward the battalion as soon as possible to a line running along trench from FITZCLARENCE FARM almost North to GLENCORSE WOOD, and to advance with the 5th Scottish Rifles on the left half of this Front to relieve the Company of 1st Middlesex Regt. and 2nd A.&S.Hrs. on the line running North and South. At first it was thought to be through final 'E' in VERBECK FARM, and later along road in rear of LONE HOUSE.

'The 4th Suffolks began moving at 10.15 p.m., and picking up the Company supporting the 2nd A.&S.Hrs. advanced to trench men-tioned (North from FITZCLARENCE FARM) which was occupied by 2 Companies, the others in shell holes in rear, by 11.30 p.m.

'The C.O. found FITZCLARENCE FARM to be only a concrete strong post of 2 rooms, 1 occupied by F.O.O. and the other by wounded, so unsuited for his Headquarters, so he therefore sent back the personnel of his Headquarters to that of the 2nd A.&S.Hrs., a strong point at J.14 central. His intentions being to return thither as soon as he had placed the Battalion on the forward line, and satisfied himself that it had been properly taken over and all ready for the further move forward, ordered to be made before Zero, so that if possible the actual advance should be made from the original approximate front line at Zero, i.e. roughly BLACK WATCH CORNER–CARLISLE FARM.

'The C.O. then proceeded to Headquarters, 1st Middlesex Regt., in a strong post just South of GLENCOURSE WOOD, [see] map, J.14.b.3.3. to meet O.C. 5th Scottish Rifles. He was not there, but he met him on his return to the Battalion. He stated that his Battalion was coming up behind him. This could be about 12.0 midnight. Fearful of being late, and as the enemy's intermittent shelling with occasional rifle shots did not decrease, the C.O. told the C.O. 5th Scottish Rifles that he would move forward at 2.0 a.m., but on reference to 98th Brigade this was not allowed. The situation rapidly became worse – the moon was gone, the shelling more regular, and a thick mist rose (or fell). About 3.30 a.m. orders or permission to advance were given if O.C. 4th Suffolk would be responsible for the whole of the 1st Middlesex and 2nd A.&.S.Hrs. front. Just then $1\frac{3}{4}$ Companies of the 5th Scottish Rifles arrived, and shortly after the remainder, some actually coming through from the East of the Line occupied. As it now seemed possible to carry out original orders an attempt was made, but terrible delays occurred, and though first 5.15 a.m. then 5.30 a.m. were fixed by neither hours had the 5th Scottish Rifles moved. About 5.30 a.m. the shelling became a heavy barrage, so that the Suffolks, who were lining the parapet ready to move in one long line, were ordered to take cover, and the O.C. 4th Suffolk tried to arrange for the advance to be made by platoons in succession from the left. This was being commenced when Zero occurred, and as the movement had not reached the 4th Suffolk he ordered the 2 front Companies to advance in platoons by rushes. The Right Companies began this, followed by a portion of the Supporting Companies, but the Left Company Commander was wounded, and, not having passed the order to any Officer, only a very small party of this Company went forward when the Right Company went. The small fragments that moved forward did well. They reached the line running North and South-West of LONE HOUSE, and the next line, BLACK WATCH CORNER–CARLISLE HOUSE, appearing unoccupied, they, after communicating with 4th King's Regt., moved into it, and did not have any casualties till they reached it from snipers of a force to the Right Front, who looked at one time as if they would turn them out. The garrison of a strong post which had held up the 4th King's Regt. shortly afterwards surrendered to the 4th Suffolk party (11 and 2 Machine Guns), and they had taken 2 prisoners on reaching the trench.

'At 12 noon the 2nd R.W. Fusiliers passed through this detachment, which then was withdrawing to rejoin Battalion Headquarters, but meeting an orderly with instructions to remain forward, they occupied a strong post near LONE HOUSE, and remained there till relieved next day by the 5th Scottish Rifles. Rations and water for 2 days were sent to them during night of 26/27th. There were two Officers with this party, Capt's Scrimgeour and Lake. The latter received a bullet wound in the wrist after taking the BLACK WATCH TRENCH.

'The C.O. 4th Suffolk remained at and near 1st Middlesex Headquarters till about 10.45 a.m., when he rejoined his Head-quarters at J.14 central, and began to reform the Battalion there as small parties came back. Some had not gone forward of the FITZCLARENCE Line; some had, and had remained in shell holes in front of it, having lost trace of their Companies and Officers in the mist and barrage, which was very heavy, chiefly from the East, but about 9.0 a.m. came from the South-East also. The main cause of some going further back was that O.C. Companies had not notified to their Companies the whereabouts of Battalion Head-quarters, and men moved West by the road running South of GLENCORSE WOOD, along which line too the wounded withdrew.

'Officers (and later the C.O.) of the 11th West Yorks Regt. came about 3.0 p.m. to relieve the Battalion, and though one had an idea that a Company was to take over the trenches the Suffolks had occu-pied and improved on North and West of Battalion Headquarters, it appeared that they were to occupy the area on a different scheme, and in the end the Headquarters of the 8th Yorks. Regt. took over Battalion Headquarters. The 4th Suffolk about 9.0 p.m. received orders to move out and withdraw to BEDFORD HOUSE area, which was done at once, and in the end the Battalion reached BELLEGOED FARM – bivouac occupied on night 23/24th – by about 12.30 a.m. 29th instant.

'Lieut. Col.,
30/9/17. Commdg. 1/4th Suffolk Regiment . . . . .'

A much more coherent account of the action comes from Lieutenant Colonel Murphy. This was first published in 1928, and the author would undoubtedly have talked to Colonel Copeman (who survived the war).

'Marching through Cassel, Steenwoorde, and Meteren, the battalion reached Reninghelst on 20th September, moving up to Bellegoed farm on the 23rd, and in support trenches the following morning, with BHQ near Clapham Junction. The enemy shelling of the area, which had been going on all day, continued throughout the night, and at daylight on the 25th reached a pitch of great intensity, extending back to Brigade Headquarters at Stirling Castle. The headquarters of two companies were hit, one twice.

'On the 25th the enemy attacked, gaining a foothold in the front-line trenches at several points. During the day these trenches changed hands more than once, and by nightfall the situation had not been restored. An attack, rehearsed at Reninghelst, had been ordered for the 26th, but as the troops detailed for it were already heavily engaged and would be unable to reach their starting-points by zero, a change of plans was found necessary at the eleventh hour. 'B' Company, during the afternoon of the 25th, advanced under intense shell-fire to the support of the 2nd Argyll and Sutherland Highlanders, who were endeavouring to recapture the front-line trenches. Not being actually employed in the counter-attack, they took up a position, in support, in a very battered trench, where they experienced a terrific bombardment and sustained many casualties. On the evening of the 25th commanding officers were suddenly summoned to Brigade Headquarters to hear the details of the new scheme. The two days' shelling had wrought great disfigurement to the face of the countryside, and Colonel Copeman, who was accompanied by Lance-Corporal G. Whiting, MM, on returning at 9 p.m., found difficulty in keeping to the track.

'Shortly after midnight the battalion took up a line running from Glencorse wood to Fitzclarence farm, having picked up "B" Company on the way. No advance could, however, be made as some of the troops on the left were not ready. Gradually the situation grew worse. The moon had gone, the shelling became more persistent, and a thick mist rose. Colonel Copeman asked the brigade to allow the 4th Battalion to go forward alone. This was not sanctioned, but at 5.45 a.m. he arranged an advance on his and the other battalion, with the men linked hand in hand so as not to lose touch in the darkness. As they cleared the irregular line of shell-holes and ditches which they were holding, down came a tremendous barrage in the face of which a regular advance was impossible. Some of the platoons, however, made certain progress. Captains Lake and S. Scrimgeour, with a score of men, succeeded in reaching the Blue Line, later making a further advance and capturing two machine-guns and fifteen prisoners, who gave valuable information. About noon a battalion of another brigade passed through and on towards the objective. Shortly afterwards Captain Lake was wounded, and the following morning Captain Scrimgeour and his party, having been relieved, rejoined the battalion. By the evening of the 27th the division had succeeded in capturing all its objectives. The relief of the division commenced in the afternoon, the battalion finally arriving at Bellegoed farm about midnight, having sustained 265 casualties, including the following officers : *Killed* : Lieut. H. C. Hattam, 2nd Lieuts. L. C. Palmer and W. P. Westwood. *Wounded* : Captain E. L. D. Lake; A/Captains S. W. Turner, MC, and G. G. B. Bannerman; 2nd Lieuts. R. Fisher, S. C. Roberts, and R. D. Hume, MC.[10']

Finally, we have the very much more human memories of Stormont Gibbs himself.

Polygon Wood

Stormont Gibbs : Of Ypres itself, Poperinghe, and the many villages that were so familiar, no memories remain. The names of hundreds of villages on the map of Northern France would be as familiar to me as places I have lived in for years yet only in the case of a very few can I visualise them or associate any particular event with them. For one visited or rested in these places after periods in the line, suffering often from extreme fatigue. One often found some sort of comfort, warmth and anyhow some semblance of civilised life. The names of these places are therefore surrounded with glamour in one's memory though no actual memory remains. Ypres one remembers better, for it was not a pleasant haven far behind the line. It was battered, no civilians were there, and most of the soldiers lived in a tunnel under the walls. It was perhaps eight miles (?) behind the front line when we arrived there in September.

One can read in a history book or memoirs, such as those of Lloyd-George, about the plan of our General Staff to take the Passchendaele ridge; one may even read, what I feel quite sure is true, that the

C-in-C and his staff did not visit the ground over which the battle they were planning was to take place. It is well known that this country was unsuited to trenches – only on higher pieces of ground could the water be kept out of them. On the low ground the Germans had made concrete 'pillboxes', usually, I should say, some fourteen to eighteen feet square. These would be defended with machine-guns which could sweep the surrounding country. Incidentally when I went on leave in early September my father told me that the *Daily Mail* had been saying that his firm (the APCM) had been selling the cement used to make these pillboxes. He and all the directors were very upset at this scandalous accusation, for they mostly had sons fighting. But looking back it seems quite likely that cement might be sold to Denmark who could resell to Germany. In fact we know that indirectly countries supply arms, etc., to their enemies – for profit.

I returned to France from leave about 19th September. I reached the transport lines in front of Ypres in the evening and went up with the rations after dark – Richards came and a string of mules and we had to follow the line of the Menin Road keeping off the road some fifty yards at one side, for the road itself was continually under shell-fire; it was quite broken up into a series of craters and only a few blackened stumps of poplars remained to show the line of where the road had been. The country we had to walk through for four miles or so was just shell holes of various size full of water and mud. It was very dark, there were many dead about, a fair stench and altogether an unpleasant contrast to the dining room at Hoppey where I had been forty-eight hours before. I remember falling over a dead man and the revolting sensation one had when this happened in the dark.

Battalion HQ was at 'Clapham Junction'. This was a most unhealthy spot on the Menin Road. We arrived and there was the 'Old Man', the Doc and Woodcock, the signals officer, and a dozen or so signallers and orderlies all crammed into a small dug-out. I was expected, so whoever had been doing my work while I was away (Paisley, I think) had remained at the transport lines ('B' Echelon as it was called). Or did P-C do my work on this occasion – I forget. I remember the CO and Doc sitting at a small table, a blanket separating them from the rest of the dug-out, in which the chief figure was Woodes, or 'Timber' as he was sometimes called, asleep on a wire bed. Oh, yes, Enraght must have been there – I could never have brought it off alone ! Timber's sergeant was better than Timber – Sergeant Bonney. And I heard directly I arrived that we were in for a show and moving off to relieve a front line battalion in a few hours. I suppose I had arrived about midnight and we probably moved off about 2 or 3 a.m. Well, we actually managed to get everybody out of that dug-out without waking Timber. How long he slept no one knows but we did not see him again for several days. It was all great fun but the joke could not be widely shared. The 'Old Man' knew I had done it, of course, and approved, but it was never mentioned. Timber probably owes his life to my childish sense of humour anyhow.

I found myself going into the line with no daylight view of the country, no time really to study the map and with all orders already got out to companies by the CO and only time to hear briefly what the great idea was. The great idea seemed to be to take the Passchendaele ridge on which effort hundreds of lives had already been squandered. Canadians had tried, Australians had tried, but the Germans still defended the ridge and it was said that on the position of the line from which we were to start there was the greatest concentration of enemy artillery yet known. I can believe it.

It was a line of broken trench by Polygon Wood – so broken that its average depth, when it could be distinguished at all, was probably about one foot. But Battalion HQ had a small dug-out with telephone to Brigade. Battalion HQ was about a hundred yards behind the 'trench' which was say two hundred yards long. On our left were the Middlesex Regiment and on our right was to be a battalion of another brigade. We were to be in position by dawn and then to advance behind a creeping barrage, find the enemy who had no definite line, storm the pillboxes and eventually get into Passchendaele if we could.

When dawn came things did not pan out as they should have done if the generals had had their way. First no one was ready except ourselves. The Middlesex had lost their way and arrived an hour late, the other battalion got quite lost and never did arrive at all. Our barrage opened as planned and immediately the enemy put down a counter barrage of such intensity that its effect was quite unimaginable. A few isolated examples of its effect may help to form some idea of it. We had practically no shelter so that the men lay flat at first, for it had been decided not to advance until the battalions on our flanks were ready. To prevent chaos and panic and simply losing the lot, the CO and I had to walk backwards and forwards along the top of the trench – at least that is what the 'Old Man' did and I had to be with him. Only the Doc remained at Battalion HQ. We were cut off from all orders from Brigade and the 'Old Man' got into a row for this and not staying in his HQ.

Well, we both had charmed lives. The CO's revolver took one piece of shell that would have killed him and I got a clod in the back that knocked me down and that was all. In fifteen minutes one regrets to record there were only two officers left with their men. The rest had simply run away and were found at the transport lines two days later, some being court-martialled. Half the men had gone similarly and most of the rest were dead. In one place where there was a short piece of unbroken trench I found six men leaning against the side in life-like positions but quite dead and quite untouched. The detonation of a shell had killed them simply by blast. The concussion in the air all round was almost maddening : one felt in torment. I do not blame anyone for running away, it was more than many people could have endured : but there is something that can never excuse running away, if you leave men behind. Officers did this and they showed how the standard of officer had fallen since the Somme took so many of our best.

It became evident that to stay where we were was doing no good so Scrimgeour and Lake OC'd 'B' and 'D' companies and took forward their men who were left. Further forward they got out of the enemy barrage. They pushed right ahead, captured a machine-gun and held their position with no support on either flank. Scrimgeour got an MC.[11]

The CO and I and the remnants of the other companies who now had no officers stayed to consolidate (if we ever got a chance to dig) and to resist any counter-attack that might develop. There were perhaps forty men with us, though in an hour I doubt if there were six.

The Middlesex battalion had for their HQ a deep and shellproof dug-out just at the left of our line where the two battalions joined. The 'Old Man' didn't like being sociable so would not even visit them let alone take a few minutes' refuge. He preferred to sit leaning up against a broken bit of concrete looking like a sphinx with shells falling all round him. There is no doubt that it gave him satisfaction to feel and to show he could stick more than anyone else – more than General Allenby perhaps, with whom he had shared a study at Sandhurst. Anyhow, it pleased him when I said I was going to spend a few minutes in the Middlesex dug-out to pull myself together. 'I am staying here,' he said. 'The sun's come out.'

I went into the Middlesex dug-out. There sat the CO and his adjutant on either side of a small table which held some whisky glasses. Both looked worn out and their faces were quite expressionless. I sat down, no one spoke and no one moved except to push a glass towards me. In the dug-out were literally heaps of wounded, some dead, some groaning and crying for water, all stinking with a stench that is to me intolerable. No one was taking the smallest notice of the wounded men. Such is war. Anyhow, what could anyone do? After three minutes of that I was for the open air and the shells once more.

When I got out I saw an officer fifty yards away running towards me – not one of ours. Suddenly his arms went above his head – there was a blinding flash I seem to remember as I was looking at him – and he seemed to jump in the air. A shell had landed just by him and strangely instead of blowing him to bits had literally blown him *up* (whole) the only time I've ever noticed that.

Then I remember seeing a tank some quarter mile back by the wood. It seemed to me we could use a tank usefully. I went back to it and knocked(!). A very scared man put his head out and I told him to get a move on and follow me. 'Can't do that, sir.' I was fed up when I thought of all the good tanks had ever done us. Here was one that might protect our flank nicely while we advanced : it might prevent our two front companies getting cut off. My hand went to my revolver and I thought, 'We'll see what about making the devil go on.' But the man hastily assured me he'd run out of petrol and proceeded to demonstrate the fact. So I left him with my curses.

Then I went to explore on our extreme right to see if the battalion that should have come had done so. I went a long way – no sign of a soul. I wondered if I might soon find myself in Hun land by chance.

Then I came to an apparently deserted pillbox. I approached it with some caution and eventually got to the entrance – no sound and quite dark inside. I had no torch. I stepped in and trod on something soft. It was a wounded Scotsman – in fact a dying Scotsman – and he cursed me. I fell forward and trod on another body and then such a wailing arose from every corner of the den – mostly cries for water and half-conscious groaning for stretcher bearers. My eyes got more used to the light and I found the floor packed thick with wounded. I don't know how long they'd been there but all were stretcher cases and unable to talk properly. Later when I told Brigade on the phone they said it was none of their business and I fear all these men were left to die. Probably the stretcher bearers who were collecting them were killed and the RAMC would never send forward as far as that to fetch wounded even if there had been someone unoccupied who could have guided them to the place.

Late that evening when everything had become quieter Scrimgeour came back to report where he was. I am very hazy about everything after that. Probably we stayed the night in the line which would have meant my second night without sleep and probably we were relieved the next day. I remember going back to transport lines and calling in at Brigade HQ, a dug-out where the Brigadier and Watson were both talking on the telephone amidst a hubbub of buzzers and signallers. They were evidently directing the operations of the new people in the line. They had only a nod for us – and we weren't interested – we'd had enough and were nearly sleeping as we walked. We had three days' 'rest' I believe before going into the line again at the same place. The first night I was continually woken up with telephone calls. The next day we had 'orderly room' all the morning: a stream of NCOs and men brought before the CO and 'reprimanded', 'severely reprimanded' or 'remanded for court-martial'. Then there was the reorganisation all to be done in very little time, the absorption of new drafts, etc. And the next day, I, as adjutant, had to prosecute at a court-martial one officer and various other ranks. A C-M is more or less run by a professional lawyer who sits beside the president and tells him what to do. The duties of a prosecutor are very nominal but none the less unpleasant. Evett, a nice fellow, who was 'made an example of' for the shortcomings of many was ordered to be cashiered. The sentence was carried out some weeks(?) later when we were further behind the line. It is one of my most unpleasant memories. The ceremony is as follows. All officers are collected – in this case in a large room. The CO walks in followed by the Adjutant. The officer to be cashiered is marched in by a guard for he is under arrest. The Adjutant is then supposed to read a lengthy document about the sins of the unfortunate officer and the sentences of the court. He then advances to the officer and cuts off his badges of rank whereupon the Sergeant of the Guard says, 'Pte X – About turn – Quick march' – and it is over. I refused to read the stuff and the CO had to – I didn't see why I should always do the dirty work. But I had to cut the poor fellow's pips off – and they wouldn't come off – it was rotten for us both.

There were two rotten little officers who deserved Evett's fate far more. They got away with an excuse but I sent them on leave and found a reason for not having them back. Funnily, they were both stock exchange men like the great Hogg in the old, old days – actually one year back but seeming ten – so long in fact that it seemed like another existence when one was very young indeed.

We probably remained for months going in and out of the line on the Ypres front but I can't remember. I only remember one other isolated event – when a damned Canadian orderly (we were relieving a Canadian battalion) pinched my beloved little revolver – which had probably seen more use than most do and had certainly saved my life and a good many others more than once (without so far as I know ever shooting anyone!).

Editor: After Polygon Wood the battalion was withdrawn to the St Omer area to re-group, returning to the front line on 17th November in Passchendaele village itself, where it suffered further casualties including two more officers killed.[12] With short periods out of the line they stayed in the Salient till the end of January 1918.

The little village of Passchendaele today is dominated by the Great

Commonwealth War Graves Commission Cemetery on the Ridge. Tyne Cot Cemetery[13] is the second largest British Military Cemetery in the world[14] and has several unusual features mainly on the personal insistence of King George V who because of its special and evocative siting took a personal interest in its construction.

Whenever I visit it, and I have been there many times, I am unable to look at the Great Cross of Sacrifice (built by the King's orders on an old German pillbox) without recalling the words of G. K. Chesterton :

> Still to the last of crumbling time
> Upon this stone be read
> How many men of England died
> To prove they were not dead.

NOTES

[1] Throughout the war Ypres was referred to by the troops as 'Wipers bloody Wipers'.

[2] Two failed to go off. One went off in 1955 killing four farmers, the remaining one is still there somewhere.

[3] No Americans saw action till well into 1918 (long after the Great German Offensive). Over one million uniformed Americans stood on the soil of France on Armistice Day of that year – the majority of whom had never seen a shot fired in anger.

[4] We now know that very few U-boats were in fact operating from these ports.

[5] It is often forgotten that at its height the 'blockade' caused by the U-boat crisis was worse in the Great War than at any time in the Second. The credit for defeating this menace must go to the Prime Minister, who fearlessly sacked senior officers (including the First Sea Lord), insisted on the implementation of the convoy system, and gave the lead to young commanders like Admiral Keyes who, with his famous 'Dover Patrol', made the English Channel an extremely unhealthy place for U-boats.

[6] Many can still be seen.

[7] It is estimated that the actual cause of death to most soldiers was drowning in the mud – a fully laden wounded man had very little chance.

[8] So named because here in October 1914 a general had sent some totally exhausted troops for a short rest before being returned to battle. The trenches here can still be seen, and there is a small but interesting World War I Museum. Sanctuary Wood was also known as Hill 62.

[9] This name was even left off the official report.

[10] Lieutenant Harold C. Hattam is buried in Tyne Cot Cemetery, Passchendaele, as is 2/Lieutenant Leslie Palmer. The body of 2/Lieutenant Walter Westwood was never found and his name is engraved on the Memorial Wall in Tyne Cot Cemetery.

124

[11] Stormont Gibbs himself was recommended for the DSO in a most astonishing and extraordinary way. The following copy of the relevant Army Form with his own notes on the back was found after his death with his Military Cross. (See page 165.)

[12] 2/Lieutenant George W. Fisher and 2/Lieutenant Kingsley C. Shuttleworth are both buried in Tyne Cot Cemetery.

[13] Named Tyne Cot by soldiers of the Northumbrian Division because the German pillboxes reminded them of Tyneside cottages.

[14] 11,500 graves.

ARMY FORM W.3121

Unit:

98th Brigade	33rd Division
1/4 Suffolk Regt. (T.F.)	VIIIth Corps.

Rank and Name:

Lieut. (A/Capt.)	Stormont
Charles Cobden	GIBBS, M.C.

Action for which commended:

Capt. and Adjt. C. C. S. Gibbs had done excellent work for the Bn. during the last half year especially during a tour in the front line from 24th to 27th September 1917 near **POLYGON WOOD** when he carried out his duties in a most thorough manner during the night of 25/26 a most trying time awaiting an advance and particularly during a barrage earlier on the 26th he was most cool and collected going continually from the Bn. to the only available telephone at some distance away to another Bn. HQ through heavy fire. In every way he was of the greatest assistance to the Commanding Officer.

Recommended by: H. C. Copeman Lt/Col. 1/4 Suffolk Regt.

Honour or Award: Distinguished Service Order

Date of Recommendation: 3/3/18
    [when Stormont Gibbs was age 20]

Notes on the reverse of the form:
This is a curious document! It is a recommendation for a D.S.O. for me in my own writing. The Colonel would not use a pen and made me take it down to his dictation. Awards were scarce in our Bn. for he never gave anyone a good write-up : the fact of his putting anyone in at all was always a remarkable event. Then I did the write-up if I got a chance and in this manner Scrimgeour and Richards got M.Cs. I don't remember anyone else getting one tho' 'other ranks' got a fair ration of M.Ms. I often wonder what the Brigade Staff thought of this thing being sent in in my writing; they never mentioned it but naturally would not have let it go forward.

Information from Army Form W.3121 found with Stormont Gibbs' medals after his death.

CHAPTER SEVEN

The Last Winter

Editor : The rejoicing at finally leaving the mud of Flanders was, however, tinged with regret. The unit had fallen foul of the re-organisers. In early 1918 the British Army was re-organised by reducing brigades from four to three battalions – this principle or 'disappearing trick' has often been used by politicians over the years to reduce the size of the Army whilst on paper making it appear the same in number of formations.

In 1918 the majority of the displaced battalions were broken up to provide replacement drafts for other battalions. A few, of whom the 4th Suffolk were one, were created Pioneer Battalions – with in theory duties as a divisional labour unit.

The pride in his unit, even under (or perhaps because of) appalling conditions has always been the hallmark of the British soldier. So it was with a genuine sense of sadness that the 4th Suffolk left 98th Brigade.

On 11th February, led by the band and drums of the 1st Middlesex Regiment, the 4th Kings (Liverpool) Regiment and the pipes of the 2nd Argyll and Sutherland Highlanders (the other battalions of the brigade), they marched out of camp at Noire Carme past their brigadier for the last time.[1]

They proceeded south to the Somme and came under orders of the 58th Division, where it was employed on road building, defensive improvements, etc.

In March came 'Disappearing Act No 2', when the battalion was reduced from four to three companies. Of this time Stormont Gibbs recalls :

Stormont Gibbs: And so we came to the winter of 1918 with its vague memories. A billet here and there, great stress with the 'Old Man', more rows, more difficulties because we had become a Pioneer Battalion. Each brigade according to the new scheme was to have one of its battalions for special use in digging and semi-RE jobs and to work when out of the line under the CRE (the chief RE officer on the divisional staff – a colonel). The Pioneer Battalion did as much fighting as the others but more digging when the others were resting – a poor scheme. The CRE and the 'Old Man' quarrelled because the latter would not do what he was told or did it wrong. The CRE used to get me to arrange things direct with him and so I got into trouble with the CO. All this had worked up to such a pitch by October 1918 that one one occasion I had to apologise to the CRE for the battalion because the CO had been so incompetent and so infernally rude to him. And a little later I told the CRE I had had all I could stick and would he insist on my going on a course to get away from it. He was very decent about it and incidentally said he thought when I returned I should find a change. He meant of course that he intended to get the 'Old Man' pushed home. Actually the change when I returned was that the war was over. But all this is premature. It is necessary to realise that in the early spring of 1918 things were getting very strained between the CO and his officers and that I was the buffer. Many who realised my foul position showed me great kindness – not least General Maitland who [in 1917] had me as acting brigade major while Watson was on leave merely to give me a holiday from it all.

It was in February, I suppose, that there was the episode of the sergeant-major in the well. Ding Dong Bell. We were in billets at a village and we drank coffee at a small *estaminet*. They were finding it hard to get enough water from this well – there seemed to be an obstruction. Our company, whose HQ were at the *estaminet*, investigated and found there was a man in the well. They made some grappling tackle but it was hard to get him up as bits came away and he fell splashing back. Eventually he was extracted and proved to be a sergeant-major swollen with the water to terrific bulk. I had to investigate his papers and the smell of his things was some smell! I wrote to his unit. He had evidently been reported missing as he had disappeared but it came out that his QM sergeant had a quarrel with him and gave him a biff on the jaw which sent him down the well. Anyhow, no one was particularly interested and we soon moved and forgot about it – though wells are not things I ever liked since.

Editor: In April also came the sad news that Lieutenant Horace Brown, MC (whose family supplied many 4th Suffolks over the years) who had been left with the old Brigade Headquarters had been killed – in an earlier letter home to his parents he had described Stormont Gibbs' winning of the MC as *'très bon'*.[2]

NOTES

[1] It is my belief that the 4th Suffolk were selected as the battalion to disappear because this was Brigadier General Heriot-Maitland's way of finally ridding himself of Colonel Copeman.

[2] Lieutenant Horace M. Brown, MC, is buried in Mendinghem Military Cemetery, Belgium.

General Sir Douglas Haig Commander-in-Chief B.E.F.

130

CHAPTER EIGHT

Kaiserschlacht

Editor : The time was now ripe for Germany to make her last great, desperate, 'make or break throw'. The total collapse of Russia had led to the transfer of all German forces on the Eastern Front to the Western, and the securing of many traditional supplies such as the wheat fields of the Ukraine. As has already been noted, 'the Yanks were coming', but they were taking an interminably long time about it,[1] so for the time being the Germans had for the first time since August and September 1914 a superiority of men on the Western Front.

Ludendorff's offensive known to the Germans as the *Kaiserschlacht* (The Kaiser's battle) because the Emperor had given the soldiers his personal assurance that it would bring victory and end the war – was planned for the beginning of the campaigning season in March. Careful strategical and tactical thinking had gone into it. On the strategic front the German High Command not only looked at the map, but considered deeply the strong/weak prop theory.

Should they deliver the knockout blow at the strong ally, i.e. the British, and then deal later at their leisure with the French, or vice versa? The former course of action was favoured because not only was it calculated that the war would be to all intents and purposes over once the British Army was defeated, but because the map also favoured it. A westward attack upon the British would force them back to the sea with very little room for manoeuvre. Thus the Somme/Arras sector was selected for the blow.

With rare exceptions, such as the capture of the Vimy and Messines Ridges, all great offensives had hitherto failed for lack of careful tactical forethought and planning. Not so this time – bringing for the first time the word stormtrooper into the language of warfare, the Germans trained in a new tactical theory of attack. Strongpoints and areas that put up unexpectedly heavy resistance were to be by-passed and 'mopped up' later; the line of least resistance was to be both followed and exploited.[2] Tactically it was remarkably effective. That it failed strategically – as we can now see it was bound to fail – was for several reasons.

Ludendorff himself, in command, proved unable to implement strategically the new tactical philosophy he preached and constantly threw his reserves at points of strong resistance instead of following the 'flowing river' of his areas of success. But that was but a bonus for the Allies. The fact was that the mechanical apparatus to keep fast advancing armies supplied just did not exist in the Great War. Using the railway systems (of which Germany had the superior) it was always possible for the defender to rush troops to the vital point whilst the attacker was always running out of steam. The mechanical advances that made it possible for Rommel to blitzkrieg across France in 1940 were just not available to the generals of the Great War.

Haig was the first to realise that there was going to be no decisive breakthrough, and thus found the key to victory, but of that more later.

The other great factor was that the hand of the Royal Navy lay heavily over this battlefield. Four years of blockade had left Germany perilously low on supplies – at home her people were literally starving. The story is told of the old professor in Berlin who on meeting sixteen-year-old twins, a boy and a girl, early in 1918, clapped the boy on the back with the words, 'Well, Hans, at least the Army will feed you before it kills you.'

Not only did the German advance finally falter for the lack of the sinews of war and the ability to transport them swiftly, but its under-nourished and by now poorly clad troops quickly became the victims of their own success. Falling upon stores of food and drink the like of which they had not even dreamed of for two years, they drank and gorged themselves stupid – even the officers fell to looting – discipline broke at a critical time, inviting and assisting counter-attack and recovery of their enemy.

A detailed account of the various attacks between March and mid-July is not the purpose of this narrative. Sufficient to say that the first and most devastating involved the 4th Suffolk.

At dawn on 21st March 1918, aided by a heavy mist, the German hordes struck at the British Fifth Army on the Somme, aiming for Amiens with its important railway junction, to divide us from the French.

Stormont Gibbs: We moved to the Oise. Our Fifth Army (Gough) had recently taken over a large piece of line from the French. The Oise was the boundary more or less between British and French, only we were responsible for the river itself. In fact Battalion HQ and two companies were on the south or French side of the river (one of these companies being in reserve). One company was on an island in mid stream and one on the north or British side of the river. We had just gone into the line here when the German March Offensive opened.

It may be remembered that we were holding (the Fifth Army) a very long piece of front so that it was sparsely manned. There was also a scheme that outposts should fall back if attacked on to a predetermined line of resistance – a scheme good enough in drill books and all right for practising on field days at Sandhurst but not so good when being chased by enemy in real life. When men retire they are liable to go on retiring and it is time staff officers learned this.

When was it – 21st March?[3] Anyhow, March. One day just before dawn I awoke to the thunder of guns – a very big affair evidently and the sky lighted up as far as we could see – and this was a long way for we were on high ground on the south bank whereas to the north it was low for miles. Strangely no shells were falling near us and I went back and rolled up in a blanket. When light came we realised the enemy were launching or about to launch a vast attack north of the river but not where we (Battalion HQ and 'C' and 'D' Companies) were. And soon we were able to look down on this drama from our place of apparent security. It was an amazing sight all that morning. The English battalions were retiring pursued by Germans. French reinforcements were sent round behind and thrown in to counter-attack and were themselves rolled back.

The fate of our 'A' and 'B' Companies seemed hopeless, though afterwards 'B' from the island rejoined us on the south bank in safety. It was a great moment seeing Catchpole when it had seemed that he and his men must have been wiped out. 'A' Company, too, did not suffer as much as they might. They held out till the people on the left gave way and in fact there was some delay, I heard, in blowing up bridges because our good Suffolks held out so long and had to be waited for. The story goes that Bodger too took them up some ammunition and suddenly found himself amongst Germans. He turned, however, and galloped to safety.

The Germans pushed back the Fifth Army so far – it was of course almost a breakthrough which might have won the war for them if properly followed up – that the French with us (Battalion HQ, 'C' and 'D' and the recovered 'B' Company) on their flank on the river left in the air in a most hazardous position if the enemy should cross the river behind us. A general withdrawal of the French Armies was therefore decided on.

Now a big retreat takes time and has to be covered by a rear-guard action. That is, someone has to stay (perhaps a battalion or more) and fight to the last man to hold up the enemy so that they cannot pursue too closely the big withdrawing army. If they are to do their job as they should they must hold their position literally to the last man and not surrender. It is a case of duty to the death.

Well, our remnants were not much use to anyone – we were quite cut off from the British Army. So it was not really surprising when a message 'Secret and Confidential' arrived just after we had finished supper. I watched the 'Old Man's' face as he read it for he had taken it from the DR. He gave his characteristic sniff and handed it to me. 'Don't tell a soul,' he said. 'Let them have a night's rest and above all don't tell the little Major.' The message read : '4th Suffolk will move into the line etc., etc. at dawn and will remain to cover the retreat of the French Army.'

I knew that night what a condemned man feels. At last we were for it and only by shirking one's duty could one perhaps be taken prisoner instead. And I couldn't talk to anyone about it. The 'Old Man' was not good company that night and I think he went to bed. It was a warm night of early Spring and a pleasant smell of earth and things that grow. I couldn't waste it in sleep. I sat out with

Enraght on the terrace of a dilapidated house where he had a shake-down. He had his gramophone and over and over again we played *The Maid of the Mountains'* 'Love will find a way'. This must always be for me the most stirring of tunes for it brings back that amazing night – and Enraght's concern because I was 'queer'. Something found a way once more. Before it was light came another order cancelling the previous one and ordering us to entrain at some station with a view to travelling (via Paris) to rejoin the British Army – this now being the only possible way.

We marched right down south into new country almost to the Marne through country where civilians and soldiers alike were all French. Finally we entrained and were taken round to Amiens and dumped down once more on the Somme to help hold up the German thrust for the Channel Ports or whatever it was.[4]

The Australians had just counter-attacked and driven the enemy from Villiers Bretonneuse and it was here that we were to go in the line. We moved into support in Gentelles Wood.

Here in the wood was Battalion HQ and one company. The CO, Doc and I took up our quarters in a small gamekeeper's hut which just had room for three 'beds' on the floor and a small table in the middle. The rest were underground in big dug-outs in the wood. The wood was periodically shelled but the CO preferred the hut. At supper a shell fell just outside. A splinter came through the brick wall and blew the handle off my revolver as it hung with my kit on a nail above where I was sitting. After supper the Doc and I paid a visit to the officers in the dug-out. Enraght had very bad toothache and submitted to an extraction by the Doc with the signaller's pliers. On the way back we found a slightly wounded cow in distress and the Doc assisted it to give birth to a calf. We then turned in for the night. In the early morning – a bang close by. The CO got out of his bed and as he did so a shell struck the wall which collapsed where he had been lying.[5] The brick and lime dust made us choke and prevented us realising at once that it was a gas shell. We breathed a lot of it – had a fearful choking feeling and then scrambled for gas masks. I got out and lay under a bush in my mask hardly able to bear to keep it on – eyes and lungs sore and feeling that one would choke.

Memory vanishes as I lie under that bush.

NOTES

[1] To be fair to the Americans – they proved themselves able to learn from experience. In the Second World War they achieved in mobilisation terms in two months what took them a year in the first.

[2] Preliminary bombardments were *short* and sharp (the opening one on 21st March was only five and a half hours), thus retaining surprise.

[3] Yes.

[4] The battalion actually camped for one night en route on the field of Agincourt; it was known to Tommy as 'Daily Mail Wood'.

[5] This shell killed Lance-Corporal G. Whiting, MM (and bar), the Battalion HQ's extremely efficient and popular runner. He is buried in Longueau British Cemetery, France.

CHAPTER NINE

Finale

Editor : By mid-July the Germans had shot their bolt – they had driven three great salients into the Allied line but the latter had held and the German Army had exhausted its strength.

The American Army was at last in the line and was now being reinforced by 300,000 men a month.[1] Large reserves hitherto held by the Prime Minister at home had joined the armies in the field.[2] The French Marshal Foch had been appointed Commander-in-Chief of the Allied Armies.[3] Now it was the Allies' turn to take the offensive.

Haig, who almost alone had kept his nerve during the dark days of March and April, was also quick to learn from the German operations. With slight modifications he now adopted their tactical methods but he also became the first of *all* the senior commanders to realise that there was never going to be a great breakthrough. Thus, in a boxing metaphor, instead of going for the knockout blow he resolved to deal his opponent an unending series of body blows that would sooner or later make his knees give way. It happened sooner.

From now on (virtually every day) battles (each of which would have made Waterloo look like a quiet vicarage tea party) were fought – each with limited objectives of a few miles, after which the forces engaged were to consolidate, re-group, re-organise, before proceeding to further offensive operations.

The greatest of these blows fell on 8th August – described by Ludendorff as the 'Black day of the German Army'. It was then that he told the Kaiser that there was no hope of victory and that peace must be made.

Everywhere the Allies' armies went forward and the 4th Suffolk went with them.[4] In action at Sailly Laurette, they took part in the 8th August battle with distinction and were reviewed fourteen days later by no less than the King himself.

In an attack on 24th August Stormont Gibbs' close friend, Captain Parry-Crooke, was wounded but continued to lead his men forward.

On 11th September their transport lines were attacked by aircraft with devastating effect (as described in the following narrative) and two officers were killed, Captain ffrench, already referred to, and the Quartermaster, Lieutenant Berwick.[5]

This is how Stormont Gibbs' war ended :

Stormont Gibbs : And so the July retreat of the Germans – following them over ground littered with their dead over all the old familiar Somme country until we were right beyond it all. We got into the line at Epehy where the Germans had made a stand. We received an order to attack an hour after we should have made the attack – not an unusual occurrence. And by the same messenger a scrawl from Bodger telling of the disaster to our poor horses and the transport and that no rations could be sent up.

There had been an air raid on the transport lines with bombs that detonated before going into the ground – specially devised, it would seem, to slice off horses' legs. Anyhow every horse was mutilated. All four officers who had been sleeping in tents were killed or wounded. Bodger, wounded in the knee, crawled round shooting his beloved horses as they lay on their backs waving torn stumps in the air. And yet people can say that wars can be justified !

A week later we were in the line again at Epehy, the CO on leave and Little Frank in command. A job to get there because if he heard an aeroplane he insisted on lying down ! When we got there our companies were taken off by guides to relieve their opposite numbers and no one knew where anyone was. No trench system. It was a dark starry night. An order came up from Brigade during the night which necessitated immediate communication with one of our companies who had not sent back an orderly to Battalion HQ to act as a guide if required. This was the occasion when I blessed the fact that

I knew how to find the Pole Star. The Company HQ was shown on my map taken over from the outgoing adjutant. It was some three-quarters of a mile away. There were big gaps between companies and if one made a bad shot one would wander right through into German lines. I knew an orderly or runner wouldn't have much chance of finding his way so I decided to go myself. I memorised the details of the map, took a direction off the star, and after twenty minutes or so of tumbling along stepped straight into the Company HQ – triumph! It was all rather important but I quite forget what it was all about.

Finally to Rougy. Arrived after a long march and men very tired. Some civilians there and a few billets – I had a good bed. Many buildings intact but intermittent shelling. There was a big school intact and the only available billet for 'B' Company but it meant the whole lot in one basket if one unlucky shell found them. The alternative was having the tired men scattered in the open. I asked the CO if I should put the company in the school. 'You decide,' he said. It could jolly well be my fault if there was a disaster. A shell came over every half hour that night. Each time I leapt out of bed to look at the school. Everyone else probably had a good night!

A few days later the CRE came to tell me there was to be an engineering course at Rouen and that I had better go and learn to make roads and railways, bridges and things – in other words have a damned good rest. In the end it was a bit of a wrench going. Just before I went a message had come that there was a bad 'flu outbreak at a village two miles away and could we send a doctor. The Doc had refused to go and I had said he ought to and we had our only row. I left him thoroughly fed up. Some days later I heard from Pip when I was at Rouen. The Doc, he told me, had taken a dangerous short cut from his aid post to the mess to avoid being late for lunch and being cursed by the 'Old Man'. A shell had caught him and taken off both his legs. His last request was not to be tied up but allowed to die quickly.[6]

And in two days came the Armistice.

Editor: Years later, Stormont Gibbs told me about the bitterness he felt over the death of the young Welsh poet Wilfred Owen, killed just a week before the war ended. Whilst he talked of Owen, I am now sure that he was thinking equally of his friend James Gaston.

Eleven a.m. on 11th November found Gibbs himself away from the battalion who were marching into Basècles to a rapturous reception from the inhabitants.

NOTES

[1] These were being brought in British ships straight from the USA to France.

[2] After Passchendaele, Lloyd-George tried to tie Haig's hands by keeping vast numbers of troops in the UK, on 'Home defence'. Facts have come to light which now prove that when he was challenged on this in the famous 'Maurice' debate the Prime Minister misled the House.

He also replaced Field Marshal Robertson (who had staunchly supported Haig) as Chief of the Imperial General Staff by the politically motivated (and as he thought Lloyd-George orientated) Sir Henry Wilson.

However, when Wilson became CIGS and was faced with the reality of the facts, he too urged the sending of men to France.

[3] This appointment was made at the request of Haig and ratified by Lord Milner on behalf of the British Government. Lloyd-George did not even know of it until Milner's return to London. In practice Foch's powers were really limited to a co-ordinating role – but it meant that Haig, who now came into his own, was able to request and get French support and co-operation in *his* offensive plans.

[4] After the recent battering it had taken on top of four years of general war-weariness and appalling waste, many feared for the fighting quality of the Army at this time. These words of Captain L. J. Baker, MC, who was with the Suffolks' 2nd Battalion, allay this fear:

'People say that the morale of the Army had gone down in those days – well, it hadn't in our Battalion. The idea of anyone refusing to go over the top was absolutely absurd – most of our troops were Suffolk men and we all had the same temperament – steady and slow, not dashing and daring. Reliable men.'

[5] Lieutenant William Berwick, TD (on loan from 5th Bn. Border Regt.) is buried with Captain ffrench in Péronne Communal Cemetery Extension.

[6] Captain James Gaston, MC, RAMC, is buried in Arras Road Cemetery, Rolincourt.

Epilogue

After the war Stormont Gibbs went up to Oxford and shortly after became creator and headmaster of Gayhurst School (which his brother-in-law Cecil Sykes who served with him in the battalion designed as the official architect) for the rest of his life. He died in harness as those who knew him well would have expected.

Adolf Hitler caused him to defect from the extreme pacifist position but the war had scarred him terribly. He certainly gave me every help and encouragement to become a regular soldier.

He talked rarely about the war – I was one of the few he would talk to – particularly when, as a young Royal Marines officer, I used to go back to see him. Starting from his genuine interest in me as a former pupil, we would discuss the theory of what I was learning with the practice of what he had experienced. He certainly expressed a wholehearted approval that the modern military were a thinking generation. Having now read his memoirs I understand even better what he felt and the reasons for the vehemence behind his remarks at the time. He lived close to G. K. Chesterton, whether he ever met him I do not know, but he would have agreed with these sentiments :

> The men that worked for England
> They have their graves at home :
> And bees and birds of England
> About the Cross can roam.
>
> But they that fought for England,
> Following a falling star,
> Alas, alas for England
> They have their graves afar.

And they that rule in England,
In stately conclave met,
Alas, alas for England
They have no graves as yet.

The Memorial to the Old Boys of Gayhurst School killed in the Second World War contains thirteen names. All of them were taught by Stormont Gibbs.

Appendix

PLACES AND LOCATIONS OF 4th SUFFOLK
AUGUST 1916 TO END OF WAR

1916	*Place*	*Trench Names*
Aug. 1	MERICOURT	
Aug. 5 – Aug. 13	FRICOURT	'Thistle Alley'
Aug. 13 – Aug. 14	BAZENTIN-LE-GRAND	
Aug. 14 – Aug. 19	HIGH WOOD	'Seaforth Trench' 'Worcester Trench'
Aug. 19	FRICOURT	
Aug. 20 – Aug. 24	MÉAULTE	
Aug. 24	FRICOURT WOOD	
Aug. 25 – Aug. 28	BAZENTIN-LE-GRAND	'Montauban Alley'
Aug. 29 – Aug. 30		'Orchard Trench' 'Wood Lane'
Aug. 31	MÉAULE	
Sep. 1	DERNACOURT	
	ALLONVILLE	
Sep. 2 – Sep. 3	CANDAS	
Sep. 4 – Sep. 5	REMAISNIL	
Sep. 5	BOUBER-SUR-CANCHE	
	MONTS-EN-TERNOIS	
	BUNEVILLE	
Sep. 5 – Sep. 8	MONTS-EN-TERNOIS	
Sep. 8 – Sep. 11	WARLUZEL	
Sep. 11 – Sep. 19	GAUDIEMERE	
Sep. 19 – Sep. 26	SAILLY-AU-BOIS	
Sep. 26 – Oct. 2	HEBUTERNE (in trenches)	
Oct. 2	ST ARMAND	
Oct. 3 – Oct. 19	SUS-ST-LEGER	
Oct. 19 – Oct. 21	CORBIE	

1916	*Place*	*Trench Names*
Oct. 21 – Oct. 23	MÉAULTE	
Oct. 23	BRIQUETERIE	
Oct. 24 – Oct. 28	TRONES WOOD	
Oct. 28 – Nov. 1		'Dewdrop Trench'
Nov. 2		'Flers Line'
Nov. 3 – Nov. 5	MONTAUBAN-CARNOY Rd. (camp)	
Nov. 6 – Nov. 9	MÉAULTE	
Nov. 9	EDGEHILL to LONGPRE to HUCHENEVILLE	
Nov. 10 – Dec. 4	CAUMONT & HUCHENVILLE	
Dec. 5 – Dec. 7	PONT RÉMY MERICOURT BRAY-SUR-SOMME	
Dec. 8	BILLOW WOOD	
Dec. 9	MAUREPAS Camp	
Dec. 10 – Dec. 11	N.E. of BOUCHAVESNES (trenches)	
Dec. 12 – Dec. 13	PETIT BOIS	
Dec. 14 – Dec. 18	N.E. of BOUCHAVESNES (trenches)	
Dec. 18 – Dec. 22	Camp 17 nr SUZANNE	
Dec. 22 – Dec. 25	MAUREPAS	
Dec. 25 – Dec. 27	S.W. RANCOURT (trenches)	
Dec. 27 – Dec. 29	Via MAUREPAS to Camp 111 nr BRAY-SUR-SOMMNE	
Dec. 29	Via EDGEHILL nr DERNANCOURT to LONGPRE then to VILLERS-SOUS-AILLY	
Dec. 29 – Jan. 19 1917	VILLERS-SOUS-AILLY	

1917

Jan. 19	Camp 12	
Jan. 20	Camp 18	
Jan. 21 – Jan. 23	HOWITZER WOOD	
Jan. 12 – Jan. 27	Front Line S of BOUCHAVESNES	
Jan. 27 – Feb. 9	Camp 19 nr SUZANNE	

1917	*Place*	*Trench Names*
Jan. 31 – Feb. 9	CLERY-SUR-SOMME (trenches)	
Feb. 9 – Feb. 11	CLERY-SUR-SOMME (trenches – in support)	
Feb. 12 – Feb. 16	CLERY-SUR-SOMME (trenches – Front Line)	
Feb. 17 – Feb. 25	Camp 19	
Feb. 25 – Feb. 27	HOWITZER WOOD (trenches)	
Feb. 28 – Mar. 4	ROAD WOOD	
Mar. 5	HOWITZER WOOD	
Mar. 6	SUZANNE	
Mar. 7 – Apr. 1	Camp 124 nr SAILLY LAURETTE	
Apr. 1	LA NEUVILLE	
Apr. 2	MOLLIENS AU BOIS	
Apr. 3	MOLLIENS AU BOIS to NAOURS	
Apr. 4	NAOURS to LONGUEVILLETTE	
Apr. 5 – Apr. 7	BEAURERAIRE	
Apr. 7	COUIN	
Apr. 8 – Apr. 11	BERLES-AU-BOIS	
Apr. 11	BLAIRVILLE/FICHEUX and 'MADELEINE REDOUBT'	
Apr. 12 – Apr. 13	Trenches N26.Co9 on NEUVILLE-VITASSE-HENIN-SUR COJEUL Rd.	
Apr. 14	Trenches BOISLEUX-AU-MONT	'Hindenburg Line'
Apr. 16 – Apr. 20	Front Line BOISLEUX-AU-MONT	'Hindenburg Line'
Apr. 20 – Apr. 22	(As April 14)	
Apr. 22 – Apr. 24	(As April 16 – Apr. 20)	
Apr. 24	BOYELLES	
Apr. 25	BLAIRVILLE-BRETENCOURT	
Apr. 26 – May 2	BRETENCOURT	
May 2 – May 10	DOUCY-LES-AYETTE	
May 10 – May 15	BOYELLES	
May 15 – May 24	Trenches	'Hindenburg Line'
May 25 – May 27	BOYELLES	

1917	*Place*	*Trench Names*
May 28 – May 31	Trenches	'Hindenburg Line'
May 31 – Jun. 20	HENDECOURT-LES-RANSART	
Jun. 20 – Jun. 24	BOYELLES	
Jun. 24 – Jun. 30	Hindenburg Line	'Shaft Trench'
	nr SENSEE RIVER	'Fop Lane'
		'River Road'
Jun. 30	BOYELLES-BEAUMETZ	
	to BASSEUX	
Jun. 30 – Jul. 3	BASSEUX	
Jul. 3	Via LA CAUCHIE, HÉNO,	
	AUTHIE to ACHEUX	
Jul. 4	ACHEUX to TALMAIS	
Jul. 5	LA CHAUSSÉE	
Jul. 6 – Jul. 31	WARLUS	
Jul. 31	ADINKERKE	
Aug. 1 – Aug. 16	LA PANNE	'Infantry Trench'
Aug. 16	COXYDE	
Aug. 17 – Aug. 20	Wellington Camp	
Aug. 20 – Aug. 22	Queensland Camp	
Aug. 22 – Aug 29	St. George's Sector	
Aug. 29	COXYDE	
	BRAY DUNES	
Aug. 29 – Sep. 1	BRAY DUNES	
Sep. 1 – Sep. 15	ZUDROVE-MOULLE	
Sep. 15	OEHTEZEELE	
Sep. 16	STEEMVOORDE	
Sep. 17 – Sep. 20	METEREN	
Sep. 20 – Sep. 23	RENINGHELST	
Sep. 23	BELLEGOED FARM	
Sep. 24	SANCTUARY WOOD	'Clapham Junction'
Sep. 25 – Sep. 28	FITZCLARENCE FARM	
Sep. 28 – Oct. 5	LYNDE	
Oct. 5	YPRES	'Shrapnel Corner'
Oct. 6 – Oct. 15	GLENCORSE WOOD	
	BIRR X Rds nr HOOGE	
Oct. 15 – Oct. 22	KORTEPXP Camp	
	nr NEUVE EGLISE	
Oct. 23 – Oct. 26	Front Line trenches	

Appendix

1917	*Place*	*Trench Names*
Oct. 26 – Oct. 30	MESSINES (in reserve trenches)	
Oct. 31 – Nov. 2	SHANKHILL HUTS, NEUVE EGLISE	
Nov. 3 – Nov. 6	Via MENIN GATE to dugouts BELGIAN CHATEAU	
Nov. 6 – Nov. 12	NEUVE EGLISE	
Nov. 12 – Nov. 16	METTETEN (MERRUS Area)	
Nov. 16	POTIJZE	
Nov. 17 – Nov. 18		'Abraham Heights'
Nov. 18 – Nov. 21	Front Line PASSCHENDAELE	
Nov. 21 – Nov. 23	POTIJZE	
Nov. 24 – Nov. 30	TORONTO CAMP BRANDHOEK	
Nov. 30 – Dec. 5	POTIJZE	
Dec. 5	Sp. Trenches area SEINE	
Dec. 6	Front Line	
Dec. 7	Sp. near SEINE	'Hamburg'
Dec. 8	Front Line PASSCHENDAELE	
Dec. 9 – Dec. 11	In support SEINE	'Hamburg'
Dec. 12 – Jan. 5 1918	STEENVOORDE-EECKE-ST SYLVERSTRE area	

1918

Jan. 5 – Jan. 10	Toronto Camp BRANDHOEK	
Jan. 10 – Jan. 12	Whitby Camp YPRES	
Jan. 12		'Hamburg'
Jan. 13 – Jan. 17	Front Line	
Jan. 17 – Jan. 19	Alnwick Camp YPRES	
Jan. 19 – Jan. 21	Toronto Camp, BRANDHOEK	
Jan. 21 – Jan. 23	Alnwick Camp	
Jan. 23 – Jan. 28		'Hamburg'

1918	*Place*	*Trench Names*
Jan. 28 – Jan. 30	St Lawrence Camp BRANDHOEK	
Jan. 30 – Feb. 11	NOIRE CARME-ZUDAUSQUES	
Feb. 11 – Feb. 14	RENESCURE	
Feb. 14	APPILLY	
Feb. 15 – Mar. 21	ROUEZ WOOD MOULINET WOOD TERGNIER CHAUNY-SUD BICHANCOURT	
Mar. 22	BICHANCOURT	
Mar. 23	R. OISE & CONDREN	
Mar. 24	BÉSME	
Mar. 25	PIERREMANDE MANICAMP	
Mar. 26 – Apr. 3	ST PAUL AUX BOIS	
Apr. 3	LE MESNIL	
Apr. 4 – Apr. 6	ST PIERRE-AIGLE	
Apr. 6 – Apr. 14	GENTELLES (trenches)	
Apr. 14 – Apr. 27		Gentelles South Dormart Line
Apr. 27 – May 7	MAISON ROLLAND	
May 7	MOLIENS AUX BOIS	
May 8	BOIS ROBERT	
May 9 – May 15		BAIZIEUX Trench system
May 16	WARLOX	
May 17 – May 31	HENENCOURT CHATEAU	'Melbourne' 'Copse' 'Court' 'Australia St.' 'Carey St.' 'Murray'
Jun. 1 – Jun. 5	BAIZIEUX	
Jun. 5 – Jun. 10	BEAUCOURT	
Jun. 10 – Jun. 17	CROUY	

Appendix

1918	Place	Trench Names	
Jun. 17 – Aug. 3	BOIS ROBERT-BAZIEUX (trenches)	'Ditton' 'Hillrow' 'Dog' 'Darwin' 'Delhi' 'Lavieville'	'Shrine' 'Derby' 'Derwent' 'Pioneer'
Aug. 3 – Aug. 5	VILLERS BOCAGE		
Aug. 5 – Aug. 7	BOIS ESCARDONNEUSE		
Aug. 7	SAILLY-LE-SEC (dugouts)		
Aug. 8	SAILLY LAURETTE		
Aug. 9	CORBIE-BRAY Rd & GRESSAIRE WOOD		
Aug. 10 – Aug. 24	BOIS ESCARDONNEUSE		
Aug. 12	Inspection by H.M. King at QUERRIEU		
Aug. 24 – Aug. 28	Trenches BOIS D'EN HAUT		
Aug. 28 – Aug. 30	Bois D'EN HAUT nr MERRICOURT		
Aug. 30	HILL 150 MARRIÈRE WOOD		
Aug. 31 – Sep. 6	MARICOURT		
Sep. 7	MOISLAINS		
Sep. 8 – Sep. 24	NURLU Trenches in EPEHY & PEIZIÈRE area	'Room' 'Poplar' 'Ockendon'	
Sep. 24 – Sep. 27	BRICQUETERIE Camp MONTAUBON		
Sep. 27 – Sep. 29	HERSIN		
Sep. 29 – Oct. 3	NORTH MAROC		
Oct. 3 – Oct. 14	CITÉE ST PIERRE		
Oct. 14 – Oct. 17	HARNES		
Oct. 17 – Oct. 18	COURRIERS		
Oct. 18	OSTROCOURT		
Oct. 19	MONS EN PÉVÈLE		
Oct. 20 – Oct. 23	AUCHY		
Oct. 23 – Oct. 26	AIX		
Oct. 26 – Nov. 9	RONGY		

1918	*Place*	*Trench Names*
Nov. 9	ROUEX	
Nov. 10	WIERS	
Nov. 11	BASÈCLES	
	BELOIR	

A NOTE ON PLACE NAMES

The reader will have noticed how many of the place names are English. This was because the Tommies not being able to get their tongues round French and Belgian pronunciations substituted their own names which stuck and even became 'official'. Thus Ploegstraat became Plugstreet.

As trench systems were dug and other places created (i.e. ammunition and stores dumps, field hospitals, etc.) in hitherto open spaces they were awarded English names usually with a strong geographical connection to the home county of the first troops there.

Tommies' sense of humour came out in the naming of the three field hospitals around Poperinghe (itself shortened to 'Pop' for the duration). Noticing how many of the local village names ended in 'hem' these became Dozinghem, Bandaginhem and Mendinghem. Both Dozinghem and Mendinghem are still the names of Commonwealth War Graves Cemeteries in the area.

Glossary

CT	=	Communication Trench
'Show'	=	An Attack/Planned Battle
RE	=	Royal Engineers
Coy	=	Company (160 All Ranks 1914)
Bn	=	Battalion (1,000 All Ranks 1914)
		Thus 2 Bn A & SH = 2nd Battalion Argyll and Sutherland Highlanders
Bde	=	Brigade (4 Battalions 1914)
Div	=	Division (3 Brigades 1914)
CRE	=	Commander Royal Engineers (at Divisional level)
CSM	=	Company Sergeant Major
A 'Blighty'	=	A wound resulting in evacuation to UK
NCO	=	Non-commissioned officer
QM	=	Quartermaster

Note on Casualty Figures

The casualty figures (and other facts) that I have quoted in this book have been derived from respectable sources, i.e. Official War diaries and eminent historians such as Sir Basil Liddell-Hart.

In practice, however, they are almost certainly not 100% accurate. We (the British) probably kept the best records of our killed, wounded and prisoners of war of any nation; but the fact that different nations had different methods of keeping (or not keeping) records, and different policies relating to their publication, is why meaningful comparison is at least extremely difficult.

To expect regimental medical officers who were often quite literally up to their armpits in blood performing amputations in appalling circumstances to pay much attention to detailed paper work is ridiculous; likewise in time of battle (i.e. of high casualties) officers such as regimental adjutants were hardly likely to give top priority to immaculate record keeping.

Russia (for example) kept, by our standards, next to no records; yet it would be absurd not to recognise that their casualties were anything other than many times greater than ours – but one is reduced to making educated guesses to the nearest million.

Many of the true facts about our enemy's WWI casualties did not emerge until records were captured in the fall of Berlin in 1945. Both Lloyd-George and Churchill were seriously misled in their histories as a result, and even men like Liddell Hart were only sniffing at the truth during the inter-war years.

How are casualties to be statistically recorded? Remember again that each nation will use its own method.

1. Killed – easy – or is it? How long after being wounded does a man have to die to be classified as killed for example.

2. Wounded – a man is wounded on say 5 separate occasions – is he counted in 5 times or once? A man who receives a serious injury on military duty in or near the battle zone but not as a direct result of enemy action – is that to be counted as "wounded" or not? Some men never reported quite nasty wounds, others would be "logged" after having a bit of plaster put over a barbed wire scratch.

3. Missing – means exactly what? Dead (body not found), prisoner of war – many presumed dead were discovered as prisoners in late 1918; or dare I say it, deserted!

4. Even deliberate falsification of figures must be reckoned with. My total inability to identify Lieutenant X referred to on page 86 leads me to believe that in all probability Colonel Copeman ordered that the incident be not recorded in battalion records. However, as the following day was one of the worst full scale battles the battalion ever endured it is possible that this incident was just overlooked.

This line of argument is endless.

Thus the ridiculous obsession with exactitude is at the best misleading and at the worst mischievous. The exact truth (like the Legend of King Arthur) will never be known. It is sufficient to say that the war was fought by millions and that in various parts of the world they perished in their hundreds of thousands.

Likewise, the order of battle of the British Army during the great war was clearly laid down. However, anyone who believes that on the day of battle brigades or battalions had the correct number of sub-units or *men* is seriously misled – thus casualties should always be viewed as a percentage of those involved : most forget that using this yardstick our casualties on the Somme were no worse than at Waterloo – both just over 30%.

I make these points here because whilst ridiculous exaggeration angers me, it is also fair to say that no historian (like the knight of old in quest of the Holy Grail) will ever achieve *his* quest of 100% accuracy.

Index

Stormont Gibbs in later years – Gayhurst School, Gerrards Cross.